Scenario Planning

The link between future and strategy

Scenario Planning

The link between future and strategy

Mats Lindgren

Hans Bandhold

palgrave
macmillan

First published 2003 by
PALGRAVE MACMILLAN
Houndmills, Basingstoke, Hampshire RG21 6XS and
175 Fifth Avenue, New York, N. Y. 10010
Companies and representatives throughout the world

PALGRAVE MACMILLAN is the global academic imprint of the Palgrave
Macmillan division of St. Martin's Press, LLC and of Palgrave Macmillan Ltd.
Macmillan® is a registered trademark in the United States, United Kingdom
and other countries. Palgrave is a registered trademark in the European
Union and other countries.

ISBN 0–333–99317–9 hardback

This book is printed on paper suitable for recycling and
made from fully managed and sustained forest sources.

A catalogue record for this book is available from the British Library.

A catalog record for this book is available from the Library of Congress.

Editing and origination by
Curran Publishing Services, Norwich

10   9   8   7   6   5   4   3   2   1
12 11 10 09 08 07 06 05 04 03

Printed and bound in Great Britain by
Creative Print & Design (Wales), Ebbw Vale

Contents

List of figures

List of tables

Foreword

The first years of the new millennium have clearly pointed to the need to prepare for the non-preparable. The dangers of failing to do this were shown in the aftermath of an insane race on the world's stock markets. ICT and telecom shares hit new highs every week, but a year later many later hit historical lows.

Could the 2001–2002 downturn have been foreseen and prepared for, and thus even been possible to capitalize on? We believe so. Much of what happened was not unthinkable; it could have been imagined. The potential problems with the 3G-launch were already clearly foreseeable in the year 2000, when European governments made big money out of the 3G race. That could have been a wake-up call for everybody involved.[1] The insane prices on dot.coms during 1999 and 2000 were another sign, and were interpreted correctly by some brave investors. And the global stock market race of the 1980s, as well as the crises that followed, could have been anticipated by using simple economic long-wave theory.

Scenario planning is a powerful tool for anticipating and managing change on an industry level or environmental level, and scenario thinking is the strategic perspective necessary in today's turbulent business environment. Scenario thinking incorporated into scenario planning is useful in almost any strategic question in today's businesses. Scenario planning is clearly the link between futures thinking and strategic action, between creative, innovative and imaginative futurizing and the more hands-on strategic planning. And strategic planning, or strategizing, without scenario thinking is more or less pointless.

In this book, our aim is to introduce the concepts of scenario thinking and scenario planning and to provide our readers with some concepts, models and tools to take back to their own companies. It is based on almost two decades of experience of scenario planning as a strategic tool, where we as consultants have guided multinationals and medium-sized companies as well as governments and non-governmental organizations in these approaches.

We would also like to take the opportunity to thank our clients and our colleagues at Kairos Future for countless inspiring dialogues. We also want to thank our families for their understanding and support during the process of writing the book.

We hope that you as a reader will find it useful. Please feel free to contact us for comments.

Mats Lindgren and Hans Bandhold

Introduction

We chose to call this book *Scenario Planning: The Link Between Future and Strategy* because scenario planning is what we do as human beings all the time. The healthy brain is constantly writing scenarios, interpreting signals in the environment and reframing them into meaningful images of and trajectories into the future. Healthy organizations do this too.

We often spend the summers cruising the Swedish archipelago. In July the narrow sounds are crowded with Swedish, Finnish, Danish, German, Dutch and even British boats, and the winds in the inner parts of the archipelago are hard to predict. The numerous islands cause constant wind shifts, both in direction and speed. As a sailor you have to be very alert so as not to lose the wind.

Amazingly there are very few accidents at sea. After almost 20 years sailing we have not yet seen any collision. The reason for this is the brain's extreme capacity to interpret huge amounts of information intuitively, to calculate the speed and direction of other boats, keep track of one's own direction and the position of surrounding banks, rocks and buoys, and at the same time prepare for alternative actions if an oncoming boat changes direction earlier than expected. All this is managed instinctively, and as a sailor I can keep an eye on dozens of boats simultaneously.

Through experience, sailors improve their ability to interpret external signals. Their brains become better and better at generating 'sailing scenarios', just as the football player over time becomes better at football scenario generation.

Without the ability to draw scenarios, and from those scenarios alternative strategies, we would not live very long. We would not be able to catch a ball, beat through a narrow sound or manage a journey on a bike. All these activities depend on our ability to observe and interpret external signals and to develop coping strategies.

ADVICE TO THE READER

The book consists of five chapters. You will be able to glance through it in 10 or 20 minutes. In a couple of hours you can do a quick read through. That is our intention. Therefore we would recommend you to read it through quickly to begin with.

Chapter 1. Why is scenario planning needed? Some reasons from the field of strategy research

In the first chapter we provide some arguments for scenario planning as an efficient method to improve performance in most companies and organizations. This chapter is based on an extensive European research project on strategy and performance in turbulent business environments. In short, we demonstrate that the combination of robust business concepts and strategies in combination with a high degree of responsiveness are the key performance drivers in turbulent business environments. Robustness and responsiveness are in turn enhanced by an organization's ability to think and play, and to foster a thinking and playing culture. Contextual awareness and thinking about alternatives are central practices to promote thinking and playing, but are far less practised than they should be.

Hence, there is a huge potential for performance improvements in most businesses, through scenario thinking and planning.

If you are not specifically interested in this topic, you could easily jump directly into Chapters 2 and 3, which form the core of the book.

Chapter 2. Scenario planning: an introductory overview

In this chapter we give a brief introduction to scenario thinking and planning, discuss its history and roots and lay a foundation for the rest of the book, specifically Chapter 3.

Chapter 3. Scenario planning in practice

In this third chapter we introduce a framework for scenario planning processes, TAIDA, giving examples from different projects. This chapter is the core of the book, and if you already have a rough idea of what scenario planning is about and primarily want to get an introduction to how it could be used in practice, you should start here and then go on to Chapters 2, 4 and 5.

Chapter 4. The principles of scenario thinking

In this chapter we develop the fundamental perspectives that scenario thinking is based on. The very cornerstone is 'drama thinking': the perspective that the future is shaped as a far-reaching play by the interactions of different actors. Other fundamentals are thinking in futures, in systems, uncertainties and actors. Finally, we also give examples of methods that could be used to improve those thinking skills. The methods are more extensively described in the appendix.

Chapter 5. The principles of strategic thinking

Scenario planning emanates from scenario or futures thinking and strategic planning. In this fifth chapter we outline some of the cornerstones of the strategic thinking needed for scenario planning. We also give examples of methods and tools that could be used.

Finally, we have put in the appendices material that could be useful, but that would make the text heavy if included in the main body. There you can find brief descriptions of some 20 useful tools, and an extensive glossary, covering most of the terms used in this book.

Why Is Scenario Planning Needed? Some Reasons from the Field of Strategy Research

For almost two decades we have worked with clients on strategy and strategic change. Numerous clients and participants in seminars and workshops have raised the question that caught our attention: 'How do you compete successfully in this endlessly changing world?'

Not surprisingly, the same question has been one of the major themes in management books, journals such as the *Harvard Business Review* and *Sloan Management Review*, and more popular business magazines. Titles like *Competing for the Future*, *Hypercompetition*, and *Competing on the Edge* were amongst the bestsellers of the 1990s. New business magazines like *Fast Company* and *Wired*, dedicated to the exploration of the business logic of the so-called new economy, have challenged old players in the business magazine market.

The general answer to the above question has been given in concepts such as 'strategic flexibility', 'strategic response capability', 'dynamic capabilities', 'dynamic core competences', 'strategic manoeuvring', 'competing on the edge', 'robust adaptiveness' and 'funky business' (Table 1.1).

In the field of more academically oriented strategy research a number of articles have been published over the past decade, addressing the question from different points of view. There are studies of the relationship between strategy and performance, decision process and performance, top management team characteristics and performance, and strategy and structure, among others.[2] However, much of the academic work is either theoretical, deals solely with specific fast-moving industries such as the IT industry or the biotech industry, or is not specifically oriented towards the new fast-changing business environments. Since more and more industries are facing the challenges of rapid change due

Table 1.1. Overview of some concepts of 'strategic flexibility'

Concept	Source
Strategic manoeuvring	D'Aveni (1994)
Strategic response capability	Bettis and Hitt (1995)
Dynamic core competencies	Lei, Hitt *et al.* (1996)
Dynamic capabilities	Teece, Pisano *et al.* (1997)
Repeated innovation	Chakravarthy (1997)
Strategic flexibility	Hitt, Keats *et al.* (1998); Hamel (2000)
OODA cycle	Haeckel and Nolan; Blaxill and Hout (1998)
Strategy innovation	Hamel (1998)
Competing on the edge	Brown and Eisenhardt (1998)
Robust adaptiveness	Beinhocken (1999)
Funky business	Nordström and Ridderstråle (1999)

to technologic developments and the dissolution of traditional industry boundaries, the restricted scope of most of the research dealing with fast-moving environments is a limitation.

To overcome those limitations we carried out a research project between 1998 and 2001 to identify strategy-related success factors in today's business world.[3]

THE SEARCH FOR STRATEGIC FLEXIBILITY: A STRATEGIC DYNAMIC TAKE-OFF

Critical to success in fast-moving and complex business environments are adaptation and speed. Lewis Carroll's story of Alice and the queen in *Through the Looking-Glass* illustrates the nature of fast-moving worlds. Alice is not moving forwards, although she is running fast, and when she notices this, the queen remarks that she must come from a very slow world. In a fast-moving world you have to run for your life just to stay where you are, and run twice as fast in order to get anywhere.

Speed is one aspect of adaptation, often emphasized as critical to success in turbulent (that is, complex and fast-changing) environments. The other aspect of adaptation is the ability to handle complexity, illustrated by Ashby's law of requisite variety (Ashby 1956). It states that the only way to destroy variety (complexity) is through variety (flexibility, adaptation).

Speed and variety are also two major themes in the litera-ture focusing on successful behaviour in turbulent business environments.

Several scholars, especially in what Lenglick-Hall and Wolf (1999) call the 'guerrilla logic school', have noted that strategic flexibility, that is the combination of speed and adaptiveness, is critical. Teece, Pisano and Shuen (1997) introduced the concept of 'dynamic capabilities' as an answer to the 'Schumpeterian world of innovation-based competition, price/performance rivalry, increas-ing returns, and the creative destruction of existing competences'. The 'reinvention capability' described above could fit into that cate-gory of dynamic capabilities, and Microsoft's ability to adapt to a changing competitive landscape is an illustration of such compe-tence (Beinhocken 1999). Chakravarty (1997) argues in a similar way when he observes that market leaders must 'repeat innova-tions, establish customer networks, sense the flow of new prod-ucts, and share responsibility for new strategy throughout the firm'. Hamel (1998) has a similar point of view when he argues for strategy innovation: 'I believe that only those companies that are capable of reinventing themselves and their industry in a profound way will be around a decade hence.'

What all these researchers and scholars are capturing is differ-ent aspects of speed, not in the notion of operational efficiency but in recognition, innovation, decision making and implementation. Table 1.1 provides an overview of strategic flexibility concepts.

DOGFIGHTS, SPEED-LEARNING . . .

The benefits of speed could be illustrated by the fighter-pilot metaphor, which surfaced the field of management during the 1990s.[4]

The United States Air Force assesses a pilot's ability to learn with the OODA Loop, a model of the mental processes of a fighter pilot. The OODA Loop is the cycle of observation (sensing environ-mental signals), orientation (interpreting), decision (selection from a repertoire of responses), and then action (executing a response). Fighter pilots with faster OODA Loops tend to win dogfights, while those with slower ones get more parachute practice. Applying the metaphor to organizations, you could say that high performers are quicker to observe changes in the competitive landscape, quicker to orient themselves in the new landscape, quicker to decide what to do, and to do it. They are quick responders.

If we apply this to business activities, the OODA Loop is closely linked to the planning cycle. The observation is the result of environmental scanning, a search for threats and opportunities, and the orientation is the outcome of the interpretation or analysis of the information. The decision is the result of a decision-planning process, and the action that is carried out implements the decision made. The OODA Loop with its business parallels is presented in Figure 1.1.

. . . AND STRATEGIC RESPONSE CAPABILITY

Flexibility is not enough, however, to enable one to respond quickly and cost-effectively to challenges and opportunities in the business environment. The 'grand challenge' to strategic management is to manage the balance between stability and flexibility. As Hitt *et al.* (1998) noted, 'Managers now face the task of creating a balance between the stability necessary to allow development of strategic planning and decision processes and instability that allows continuous change and adaptation to a dynamic environment.' The downturn on the global stock markets during the first

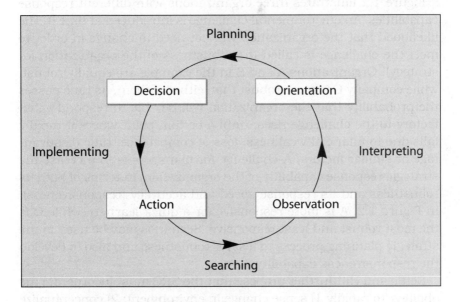

Figure 1.1. Illustration of the OODA Loop

years of the new millennium and the collapse of some of the most respected companies are clear illustrations of this.

In a theory paper, Richard Bettis and Michael Hitt develop the concept of what they call 'strategic response capability', a capability that besides responsiveness also includes strategic robustness. Their concept was based on an analysis of the changing competitive landscape with more intense and unpredictable competition, the dissolution of traditional industry boundaries, and the cry for redefinition of organizations and organizational learning. 'Because of the dynamism in the new competitive landscape, firms cannot remain static even if they operate in mature industries. . . . Thus, firms in the new competitive landscape must achieve dynamic efficiency often regardless of their industry's life cycle. As such, managers must have an entrepreneurial mindset, emphasizing innovation in most industry settings' (Bettis and Hitt 1995: 14).

According to Bettis and Hitt, the strategic response capability can be compared to the stimulus–response paradigm of biology, where the capability of an organism to respond to stimuli in the environment is the key determinant of its fitness for survival. Thus, it consists of two components: the ability to respond to threats and the ability to search actively for better positions in the environment and to exploit new opportunities.

Figure 1.2 illustrates three organizations with different response capabilities. An environmental challenge is introduced at time 0. The likelihood that the organization will not need to change in order to meet the challenge is called the robustness of the organization (or strategy). Organizations A and B in the example are equally robust, while company C is more robust than either of them. As time passes the probability that the organization will be able to respond satisfactory to the challenge rises, until a certain point where it rapidly falls due to financial weakness, loss of competence, time disadvantage or similar factors. A challenge for managers is to increase the strategic response capability of the organization, in terms of both its robustness and its response speed and accuracy (responsiveness). In Figure 1.2, A is more responsive (or a quick learner), while C is the most robust and least responsive. Scenarios may be used in the strategic planning process to test for robustness and also to develop the responsiveness capability.

Bettis and Hitt further propose that the SRC must incorporate the abilities 'to rapidly 1) sense change in environment; 2) conceptualize a response to that change; and 3) reconfigure resources to execute

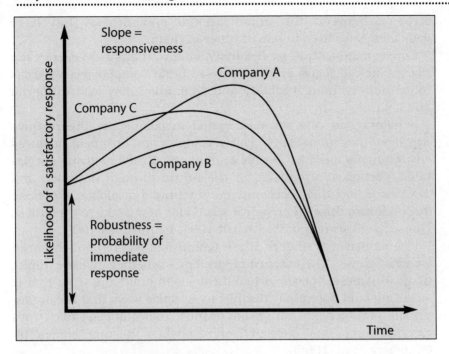

Figure 1.2. Illustration of the strategic response capability
Adapted from Bettis and Hitt (1995).

the response' (1995:16). The parallel to the OODA Loop is obvious. 'Sense' is parallel to 'Observe'. 'Conceptualize' is similar to 'Orient and decide'. 'Reconfigure and execute' equal 'Action'.

Bettis and Hitt finally conclude, 'further work is needed to develop an overall package of specific mechanisms for shifting the strategic response curve upwards' (1995: 16). An open question is whether there also is a need for a package to increase robustness.

PUTTING THE STRATEGIC RESPONSE THEORY INTO PERSPECTIVE

By incorporating the robustness concept, Bettis and Hitt (1995) have captured the essence of life. From a biological or ecological point of view, the general theme in organizational life is the struggle between life and death, or exploration and exploitation (Normann 1975; March 1996). There seems to be a constant flow and need to balance between those two states, and a constant struggle between the organizational subcultures that have dedicated their lives to one or other of them.

Consequently, strategic flexibility without robustness carries the risk of lack of focus and inability to build competence, whereas robustness without flexibility and adaptation may lead to inertia and death.

Scholars and practitioners rooted in complexity theory have explained that robust strategy in a complex and turbulent business environments must be flexible and adaptive. Just as living species build 'portfolios' of options for the future through mutation and 'DNA experimenting', corporations must build portfolios of options for the future through an active search for new peaks in the fitness landscape (Brown and Eisenhardt 1997; Beinhocken 1999).

In a similar way, James Brian Quinn has pointed out the need for robustness: 'The essence of strategy – whether military, diplomatic, business, sports, [or] political – is to build a posture that is so strong (and potentially flexible) in selective ways that the organization can achieve its goals despite the unforeseeable ways external forces may actually interact when the time comes' (in Mintzberg *et al.* 1995).

SO HOW MUCH DOES STRATEGIC FLEXIBILITY MEAN?

In order to test the importance of strategic flexibility to performance we defined two concepts – robustness and responsiveness – in line with Bettis and Hitt's work (1995). A questionnaire was sent to a random selection of companies in Sweden, Great Britain, Germany and the Netherlands. The companies came from three sectors: banking and insurance, the media and ICT. Responses were received from 105 companies, mainly from CEOs.[5]

Robustness, or strategic robustness, was defined by Bettis and Hitt as 'the potential for success under varying future circumstances or scenarios'.

Responsiveness, or strategic responsiveness, was defined by Bettis and Hitt as the ability 'to rapidly 1) sense change in environment; 2) conceptualize a response to that change; and 3) reconfigure resources to execute the response'.

Performance is defined and measured in numerous ways in management research. Bettis and Hitt define performance vaguely, or broadly. Thus, performance in this study was defined as overall output performance, or the combination of financial performance, business, and organizational effectiveness, and the ability to successfully invest in future capabilities.[6]

Environment is a key variable in management research performance.[7] Bettis and Hitt discuss complex and rapidly changing environments, often referred to as turbulent environments. But what some researchers call turbulent, others call dynamic (Hart and Banbury 1994). To avoid confusion in this research the word 'raplex' (rapid and complex) will be used for environments that are both rapidly changing and complex. Thus, a raplex environment is a *rapidly changing, complex and unpredictable* environment.

IT MEANS MORE THAN WE THINK!

So how much does strategic flexibility mean? The direct answer is that it means far more than we generally imagine. The results from the analysis indicate that strategic flexibility (the combination of robustness and responsiveness) explains between 60 and 70 per cent of the performance differences between companies, and between 20 and 40 per cent of the differences in financial performance.

Responsiveness was found to be relatively more important to overall performance than to financial performance. This may be because responsiveness is closely linked to entrepreneurial innovative and expansive behaviour that improves quality, growth, motivation and other non-financial performance indicators, and thus total performance. On the other hand, such expansionist behaviour often negatively affects financial performance in the short run.[8]

However, results also indicate that responsiveness (similar to a more limited definition of strategic flexibility) is no more important than robustness.[9] In fact, in highly raplex environments, the relative importance of robustness increases for total performance and becomes as important as responsiveness. In fact, for financial performance, robustness is more important than responsiveness. That robustness is more important in a raplex environment might at first sound counterintuitive. One explanation could be that well-crafted business concepts, clear and robust goals and principles, help the organization to focus on tasks and may even enhance innovation and improvisation in raplex environments. Brown and Eisenhardt's (1997) findings from computer industries support such a conclusion. In a multiple-case study, they found considerable differences among firms, with the high performers marked out by clear and robust organization, communication patterns and goals. Consequently, those organizations could concentrate on experimentation and projects, while the low performers were stuck in mess and confusion caused by a 'rule breaking' culture and lack of structure. In a recent article, Peter Doyle (2000) also supports the proposition that robust strategies based on long-term focus, corporate effectiveness, and commitment and empowerment are critical to long-term performance in raplex environments.

Another reason for the increased importance of robustness could be that the more raplex the business environment is, the more important differentiation becomes.[10] But at the same time differentiation becomes harder since it becomes less simple to match internal capabilities with external demands and opportunities, and since it is hard to find concepts that provide more than temporary competitive advantage in such environments. That might be the reason why many companies fail with their differentiation strategies (Gelatkanycz and Hambrick 1997). Thus, those who are capable of defining and redefining robust, hard-to-copy, core-competence-based differentiation strategies will be able to gain a sustainable competitive advantage.[11] A real-world illustration of the consequence of lack of robustness is the dot.com collapse in the year 2000. Many of the dot.coms were unable to find robust concepts and relied only on being first in the field. But that has often proved inadequate.

Practical implications for managers in raplex environments

The point of departure for this research was the real-world question: 'How do you compete successfully in this endlessly changing world?' The most obvious practical implication of the findings is the need for managers to emphasize robust hard-to-copy business concepts and strategies, without neglecting the need for responsiveness. Improving the robustness of the business concept and organization requires thorough analysis and bold decisions. It requires strategizing and thinking things through to the deepest possible level (Hamel 2000).

The ideal situation in raplex environments seems to be a combination of robustness and responsiveness, where thoroughly crafted business concepts and organizational principles provide a lasting framework that the organization can rely on. The concept sets the rules, and the organization is free to improvise and experiment itself into the future, following those basic rules. Hitt describes this in the following way: 'Managers now face the task of creating a balance between the stability necessary to allow development of strategic planning and decision processes and instability that allows continuous change and adaptation to a dynamic environment' (Hitt *et al.* 1998: 24). Williamson, rooted in complexity theory, concludes: 'In the face of uncertainty and rapid change, companies must reengineer their strategy processes to create a portfolio of options for the future and integrate planning with opportunism' (1999: 117). And Collins and Porras say: 'Companies that enjoy enduring success have core values and core purpose that remain fixed while their business strategies and practices endlessly adapt to a changing world ' (1996: 65).

There seems also to be an evolutionary process in the balance between robustness and responsiveness (Figure 1.3). With a high degree of responsiveness a company can create a competitive

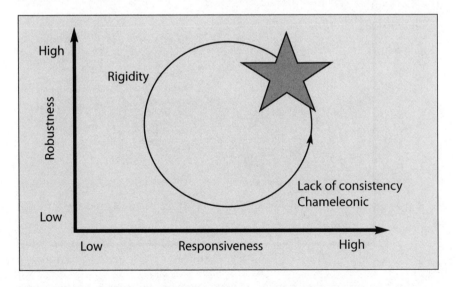

Figure 1.3. The key challenge to business leaders is to manage the balance between robustness and responsiveness and to avoid vicious circles

advantage that can be deployed into robust business concepts or core competences. Being able to create such an advantage tends to shift the organizational focus towards incremental change and development of already existing competences, products and so on rather than pure innovation. Slowly the organization slips over to the upper left corner of Figure 1.3, with very robust concepts, but with ever lower responsiveness. However, this is not a stable position. Eventually, new technology or new entrants will erode the robust position and the organization will tend to slide into the lower right corner. The vicious circles are those that at each turn of the wheel nudge the organization to ever lower levels of robustness and responsiveness. The virtuous circles are those where consecutive 'cultural revolutions' lead to higher and higher levels of robustness and responsiveness, slowly expanding the strategic repertoire and time horizon and driving the organization from the 'cleaning' position to a shaper role (Figure 1.4).

The balance between robustness and responsiveness is very similar to what is needed in jazz improvisation or jamming (see Figure 1.5).[12] When jazz groups are jamming, they follow some

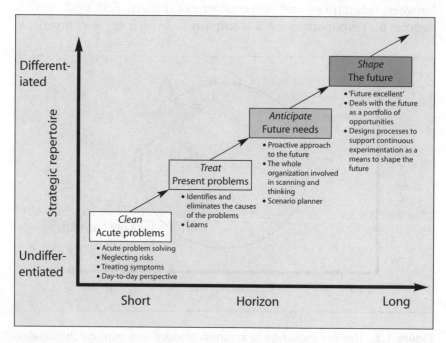

Figure 1.4. Four levels of proactiveness: from cleaner to shaper

- Robust structure –
  a precondition for
  swing
  - Tune, harmony, rules
  - Beat = backbone
- Personal mastery and
  experimental search –
  precondition for
  exploration
  - New paths
  - New highs
  - New harmonies

*'If it doesn't swing –
shoot the bassist'*

Bertil Strandberg, world trombonist

Figure 1.5. There are several similarities between successful companies and a jam session

basic rules: a sequence of harmonies, a beat steadily kept by the bassist, and so on. The bass is the base. But above it there are improvised solos searching for new possibilities, new harmonies and new expressions. To continue this metaphor, as the pace increases, the more important it is, that the bassist keeps the beat.

And as the world-renowned trombonist Bertil Strandberg (personal conversation, 1997) says: 'If it doesn't swing, shoot the bassist!'

Or, to follow the words of John Kao: 'Jazz – like business – implies a series of balancing acts. It must always be disciplined – but never driven – by formulas, agendas, sheet music. It must always be pushing outward, forward, upward – and therefore, inevitably, against complacency' (1997: 29).

WHAT MAKES COMPANIES STRATEGICALLY FLEXIBLE?

The natural question that arises from the conclusions above is: 'Why are some companies more strategically flexible: what do they do differently?' To be able to answer that question we conducted a comprehensive literature review of the field of strategy and performance in raplex business environments and came up with a dozen of possible explanations related to top management, organizational structure, strategy process and chosen strategy. These were operationalized into multiple-item questions and included in the questionnaire described above.

When we analysed the results we found that most of our hypotheses were verified. Companies emphasizing strategic planning are both better performers and have a higher strategic flexibility than those that do not. The same is true for those that have a proactive experimental/entrepreneurial strategy, and those that ban back scratching and office politics in the top management team and elsewhere.

Even more interestingly, when we analysed the individual sub-questions we found that they basically fall into three dimensions, and that the dimensions are almost equally important for overall performance and for explaining strategic flexibility. We could call the three dimensions: 'Thinking', 'Playing' and 'Gardening' (see Figure 1.6). Each dimension accounts for between 25 and 35 per cent of the total performance in raplex environments.

Organizations that are strong in the thinking dimension establish a mental lead. They anticipate change earlier than others through

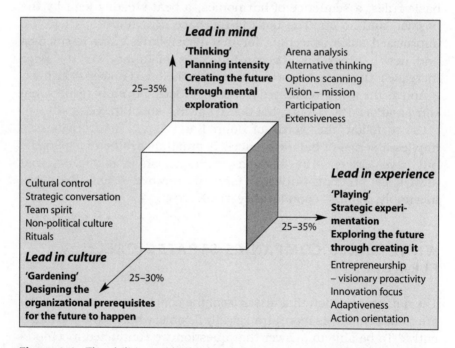

Figure 1.6. The abilities to 'think, play and garden' are the three organizational behaviours that most strongly predict performance in turbulent business environments

arena analysis, alternative thinking (scenario analysis etc.) and environmental opportunity scanning. In that sense they are strategic.

Organizations skilled in the playing dimensions are the entrepreneurs. They are visionary and proactive, emphasizing innovations, adaptive and non-formalistic. While the thinkers explore the future theoretically, the players do it in practice, through continuous innovation and experimental products. They try to predict the future by creating it.

The 'gardening' dimension is first of all a supportive dimension. The skilled gardeners are good at controlling and developing the organization through cultural control, in other words through the thorough design of remuneration and other feedback systems that support the chosen strategy. They emphasize and support strategic conversation in the organization, and avoid office politics.

When we consider different combinations of thinking, playing and gardening capabilities, we quickly realize that the three dimensions are all equally necessary for a healthy company. That is, they must to some extent be in place. As illustrated in Figure 1.7 an organization with high thinking skills but low playing capability will fail to

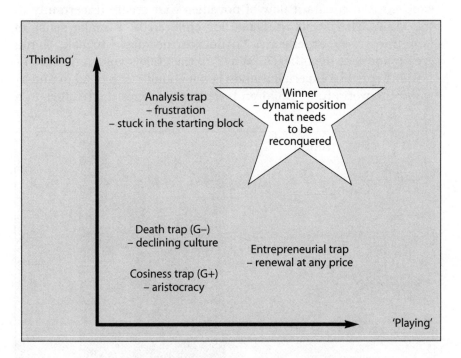

Figure 1.7. Different types of organizational anomalies

accomplish anything but plans. They will be stuck in the analysis trap. Those are the companies that never are taken by surprise, but nevertheless constantly fail to take advantage of their insights. On the other hand, companies stuck in the entrepreneurial trap will emphasize change at any price. Many of the dot.coms and Internet consultancies of the late 1990s fell into that category. They were so obsessed with change and new business concepts that they failed to develop any fundamental and robust business strategies at all.

The coziness trap can be found in organizations living in regulated markets, whether private or public. There is no need for either thinking or playing, but there can still be much emphasis on developing an intellectually and spiritually encouraging culture. The most dangerous of all the anomalies is the death trap. No organization survives for more than a short period in that position.

Like a child?

To use a metaphor, one could say that a successful organization is like a child. A child, like a turbulence-exposed company, is exposed to a constant flow of novelties that create uncertainty in the brain. The grand challenge for children is to make sense of everything they experience. To do so, they have to ask, think, create and test hypotheses. 'Why?' is the child's golden question.

But theoretical experimentation is not enough for a child to understand the world fully. Children have to experience the realities in a

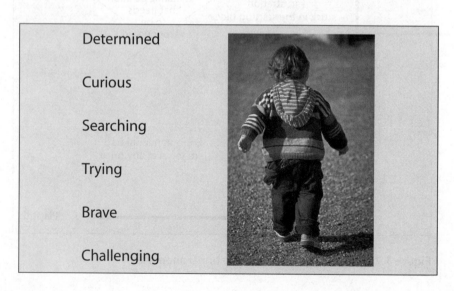

Determined

Curious

Searching

Trying

Brave

Challenging

more concrete sense too. 'Does mum really mean no, when she says no? I've got to try!' 'What is this stuff – what does it taste like?' 'What happens if we mix these things together?' In learning, children have to question the 'laws' and to find out things for themselves in order to really own the world. And the same is true for a successful company that not only wants to be a leader in the old regime, but that also wants to be around when the new regime breaks through.

Finally, a successful company also has the qualities of a good parent: the mother or father who provides a robust framework to rely on, guides the kids through role-modelling, and supports and even directs questions, questioning and experimentation.

SO: ARE COMPANIES EMPHASIZING THE ESSENTIALS?

Having said that thinking, playing and gardening are the three golden practices in the raplex world, the natural question is: 'To what extent do companies exercise them?' Let us frame the answer in the following way: there is a huge performance potential for most companies! Or, more to the point, in general, some of the most important practices are not heavily exercised. As you can see in Figure 1.8, that is true for most of the thinking-related practices such as arena analysis, opportunity scanning, alternative thinking, extensiveness and participation. It is also true for the most important of the playing practices, namely visionary proactiveness, and it is true for the most important of the gardening practices, cultural control.[13]

Since in this book we are specifically interested in practices relating to scenario planning, it is worth noting that five of the six practices most closely related to scenario planning fall into the upper right corner: that is, skills that are important but not very widely practised.

THERE IS NEED AND THERE ARE OPPORTUNITIES

The aim of this outline of the book has been to give some research-based evidence of the need for and the potential of scenario thinking and planning. As we have shown, there is strong evidence that the combination of robust business concepts and a responsive

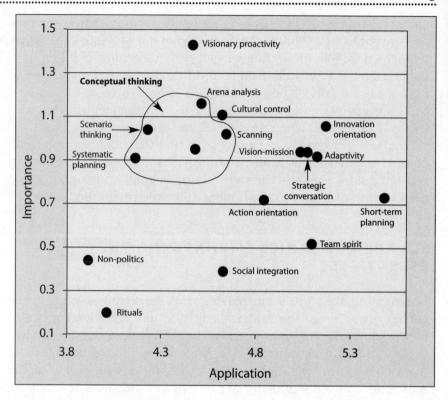

Figure 1.8. The diagram illustrates that most companies have a huge performance potential through a stronger emphasis on thinking-related practices

organization is the key to performance in more turbulent or raplex business environments that almost every company today faces. There is also strong evidence (although we have presented only a small part of it here) that robustness and responsiveness are strongly driven by three competences that we can identify as thinking, playing and gardening. The thinking practices have the highest impact on robustness and responsiveness, and thus on organizational performance; they are the strategy-related practices that fall under the label of 'scenario planning practices', namely arena analysis, opportunity scanning, vision and mission, alternative thinking, extensiveness and participation. Finally, we have seen that it is often these very potent approaches that are practised least by companies in general. It is not hard to believe that tomorrow's winners will be those who grasp this golden opportunity to leave the field behind.

Scenario Planning: An Introductory Overview

WHAT ARE SCENARIOS AND SCENARIO PLANNING?

What is a scenario? Are all descriptions of the future scenarios? And what can scenarios be used for?

There is no single definition of either scenarios or scenario planning. Different thinkers have made their own definition of scenarios and scenario planning:

- 'An internally consistent view of what the future might turn out to be' (Michael Porter 1985).
- 'A tool [for] ordering one's perceptions about alternative future environments in which one's decision might be played out right' (Peter Schwartz 1991).
- 'That part of strategic planning which relates to the tools and technologies for managing the uncertainties of the future' (Gill Ringland 1998).
- 'A disciplined method for imaging possible futures in which organizational decisions may be played out' (Paul Shoemaker 1995).

It is clear from these definitions that a scenario is not a forecast, in the sense of a description of a relatively unsurprising projection of the present. Neither is it a vision, that is, a desired future. A scenario is a well-worked answer to the question: 'What can conceivably happen?' Or: 'What would happen if. . . ?' Thus it differs from either a forecast or a vision, both of which tend to conceal risks. The scenario, in contrast, makes risk-management possible.

It is also clear that scenario planning is not only about scenario writing, but something more, something more closely related to strategic planning. We will come back to that later.

....

We all play about with scenarios. Healthy minds are always generating scenarios for the immediate future. The brain thinks ahead and processes information about what is to come.

All living organisms such as human beings or organizations need a properly functioning feedback system to let them know what has happened. We need to learn from what we have done. But to be able to choose which way to go, we also need information about the future. We need 'feed-forward' systems (see Figure 2.1).

Even if the mind is continually creating scenarios, it is less common for us as individuals or companies to work on them systematically. Most scenario planning in companies and organizations attempts to imagine or calculate the effects of alternative decisions. We ask ourselves what may be the effect of, for example, a certain deal or a move by a competitor. However, systematic work on scenarios of the outside world is definitely rare. One reason is that it requires more time and knowledge. If scenario planning is not simply to be a pleasant exercise, someone in the organization must be responsible for continuity, and one or more people for drawing conclusions from the exercise and working out its consequences for the choice of strategies and so on.

Scenarios and other futures

We have said that scenarios are different from forecasts, prognoses and visions. Scenarios are vivid descriptions of plausible futures. Figure 2.2 illustrates the differences between the three main categories of futures. In general, the further ahead we look, the greater

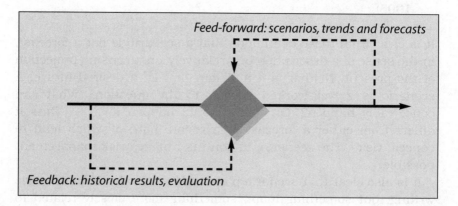

Feed-forward: scenarios, trends and forecasts

Feedback: historical results, evaluation

Figure 2.1. Feedback: historical results, evaluation

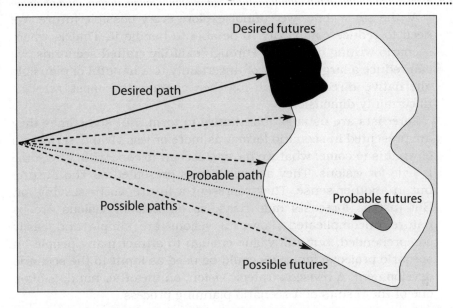

Figure 2.2. The relations between possible, probable and desired futures

the possibilities. From a personal point of view for instance, I do not have that many options within a one-week time frame. The number of possible 'one-week futures' is limited. But if I look five, ten or even more years ahead the number of alternatives is much greater. Some of the possible futures seem today more probable than others. Others are preferable, more desirable, and the desired futures could often differ from the most probable ones. The most desired future, my own vision of how I would like to live my life, might not even fall within the field of 'possible' futures.

In terms of planning we constantly make plans that include forecasts as well as scenarios and visions, both as individuals and as organizations. As organizations we often rigorously plan with different types of forecast and projections. Under stable conditions and with short timeframes, forecasts are both necessary and powerful. We need risk reduction and certainty to be able to make decisions. And that is what the forecasts provide.

However, the further ahead we look, and the more complex the systems we try to predict, the more irrelevant this type of planning becomes. As uncertainty increases we need other planning tools to uncover and explore the future business environment in order to identify potential risks and opportunities, and to prepare for not one but many possible futures.

At the same time, we cannot explore every possible future. We need to reduce complexity to be able to handle it. That is where scenario writing comes in. Through skilfully crafted scenarios, we can reduce a large amount of uncertainty to a handful of plausible alternative directions that together contain the most relevant uncertainty dimensions.

Forecasts are usually quantitative in form. But sometimes they are presented in scenario format as more or less vivid descriptions of what is to come: what we have to accept, to cope with. The same is true for visions. They are sometimes presented as The Future, but in another sense. They represent a future worth striving for. But just as forecasts hide risks, so do visions. Visions are by nature uncomplicated. Powerful visions are simple and easily comprehended, but still vague enough to attract many people. In scenario projects, forecasts could be used as input to the scenario development. A revised strategic vision, on the other hand, is often one of the results of a scenario planning process.

Scenario planning: learning tool and planning instrument

Scenario planning is, as we've seen, an effective strategic planning tool for medium to long-term planning under uncertain conditions. It helps us to sharpen up strategies, draw up plans for the unex-

Table 2.1. Differences between scenarios, forecasts and visions

Scenarios	Forecasts	Visions
Possible, plausible futures	Probable futures	Desired future
Uncertainty based	Based on certain relations	Value based
Illustrate risks	Hide risk	Hide risk
Qualitative or quantitative	Quantitative	Usually qualitative
Needed to know what we decide	Needed to dare to decide	Energizing
Rarely used	Daily used	Relatively often used
Strong in medium to long-term perspective and medium to high uncertainties	Strong in short-term perspective and low degree of uncertainty	Functions as triggers for voluntary change

pected and keep a lookout in the right direction and on the right issues. But scenario writing is not only a planning instrument. It is also an effective learning tool. Thinking in scenarios helps us understand the logic of developments, clarify driving forces, key factors, key players and our own potential to exert an influence. Scenario planning is future planning in an era when traditional strategic planning is obsolete (Mintzberg 1994).

In fact, scenario techniques can be used for several purposes, as we will see later. In Figure 2.3 we illustrate the dimensions we have discovered over the years of using scenario techniques in various projects. Sometimes scenarios are clearly used for planning reasons with an explicit aim to develop practical results. Industry, technology or consumer scenarios can guide R&D, business or product development. Scenarios may function both as inspirations for generating idea and as filters through which new ideas and projects can be passed. In these cases scenarios function within a 'new business' process. But they can

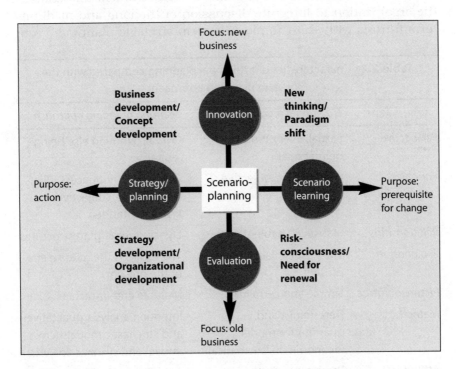

Figure 2.3. Scenario projects could be used for different purposes and with different focuses

also be used for evaluation purposes, for instance to test existing business concepts, strategies or products.

At other times scenarios may be used for learning or to drive change. Scenarios are powerful in challenging existing paradigms and assumptions, especially for those who are involved in the scenario generation. Therefore, scenario workshops are powerful instruments in the process of challenging existing paradigms and creating shared perspectives on the future. In Chapter 3, Scenario planning in practice, we will describe that more thoroughly.

Scenario planning: the link between futures studies and strategy

Scenario planning is, as we have seen, a planning method used to deal with uncertainties in the future business environment. The differences between traditional strategic planning approaches and scenario planning are illustrated in Table 2.2.

It is obvious that scenario planning is an instrument that enables the organization to integrate discussion of the long and medium-term futures with short to medium-term strategic planning. From

Table 2.2. Characteristics of traditional planning compared with the scenario planning approach

	Traditional planning	*Scenario planning approach*
Perspective	Partial, 'Everything else being equal'	Overall, 'Nothing else being equal'
Variables	Quantitative, objective, known	Qualitative, not necessarily quantitative, subjective, known or hidden
Relationships	Statistical, stable structures	Dynamic, emerging structures
Explanation	The past explains the present	The future is the *raison d'être* of the present
Picture of future	Simple and certain	Multiple and uncertain
Method	Determinist and quantitative models (economic, mathematical)	Intention analysis, qualitative and stochastic models (cross-impact and systems analysis)
Attitude to the future	Passive or adaptive (the future will be)	Active and creative (the future is created)

that perspective a scenario planning process consists of two phases linked by the scenarios built during the first phase (Figure 2.4). Each phase consists of several stages, some more creative or intuitive, others more analytical.

When should scenarios be used as a tool in strategic planning? The simple answer to that questions is: 'When there is a reason.' And there is a reason to use scenarios in the strategic process as soon there is a significant amount of uncertainty in the decision context. Scenarios are particularly valuable when it comes to paradigmatic or non-linear change, for instance when product categories are reaching a level of 'over-maturity' and need to be replaced with something new, or in the face of rule-breaking competition that is creating a new business logic (Figure 2.5). This is not the kind of change that traditional linear planning is suited for, but is the home ground of scenario planning.

This leads to the conclusion that, particularly in uncertain times, there is a need for a higher level of strategic thinking that integrates the uncertainty-based futures thinking (scenarios) and more traditional strategic planning methods in order to cope with challenges in business environments, and to be able to exploit the opportunities created (Figure 2.6). In reality, scenario development often lives its own life, separated from strategic planning. That makes futures thinking a purely intellectual exercise, and strategic planning (at best) planning within an existing paradigm. Sometimes that is enough, but often not.

In today's endlessly changing world, operational or process integration is not enough. We also need strategic integration,

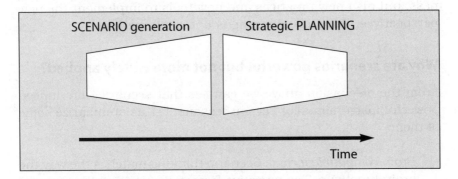

Figure 2.4. Scenario planning is the combination of scenario analyis for strategic purposes and strategic planning based on the outcome of the scenario phase

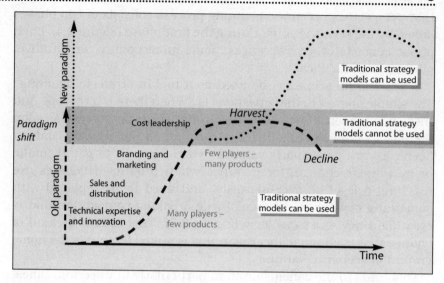

Figure 2.5. Scenario planning is well suited to the task of dealing with paradigmatic, non-linear change

which requires corporations to consider the synergies between different products, technologies, markets and the like, and often to redefine the business concept (Figure 2.7). However, strategic integration is basically concerned with the recombination and re-invention of the present. Beyond that, corporations increasingly need what we could call a futures integration, that is, to integrate future trajectories into day-to-day business planning. As we saw in Chapter 1, this is the prerequisite for future excellence. Futures integration requires not only a new perspective on business, but also new practices and new tools to implement the new perspectives. Scenario planning is one such method.

Why are scenarios powerful but not more widely applied?

From the discussion above we can see that scenarios are indeed powerful instruments for several reasons. Let us summarize some of them:

- *Brain-compatible format.* Scenario thinking matches the way the brain functions. The narrative format of scenarios (images and stories) makes them easily memorable. What you can visualize, you can also believe.

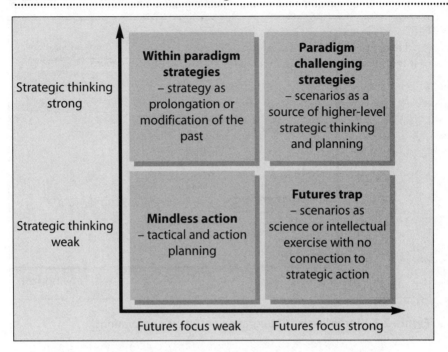

Strategic thinking strong

Within paradigm strategies
– strategy as prolongation or modification of the past

Paradigm challenging strategies
– scenarios as a source of higher-level strategic thinking and planning

Strategic thinking weak

Mindless action
– tactical and action planning

Futures trap
– scenarios as science or intellectual exercise with no connection to strategic action

Futures focus weak   Futures focus strong

Figure 2.6. Development of paradigm-challenging strategies requires an integration of high-level strategic thinking and a strong emphasis on futures thinking

- *Opening-up of divergent thinking.* A set of scenarios should represent qualitatively different futures. By forcing your mind to think about qualitatively different directions, you train your capability to think the unthinkable, and thus improve your ability to foresee unusual events. The open format, with no 'right' or 'wrong', also assists shared exploration of the future.
- *Complexity-reducing format.* Through scenarios, complex business or general environments can be reduced to a manageable amount of uncertainty. They facilitate complexity reduction without over-simplifications.
- *Communicative format.* Scenarios are easy to communicate and to discuss. A shared set of scenarios within an organization provides a common language and world view that simplifies decision making.

But if scenarios are that powerful, why haven't they been more widely used? There are at least four reasons for this.

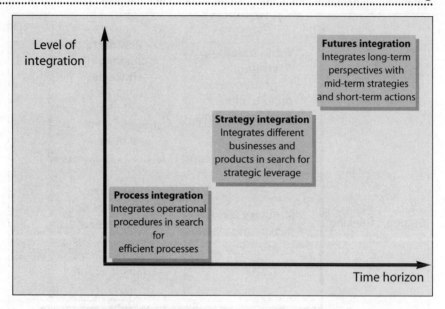

Figure 2.7. Three levels of integration in today's corporations

- *Uncertainty in conclusions.* Scenario planning does not give one single answer about the future. Therefore it does not provide the security that is often required in decision making. Scenario planning is a much more demanding process than traditional planning.
- *Counterintuitive to managerial simplicity.* Another aspect of the scenario output is that scenario planning does not accord with the managerial simplicity that says that there is one right answer to every question, that every problem can be divided into three parts, and that each part can be solved separately. Scenario planning is a more holistic or systemic approach to planning than traditional methods.
- *Soft methods and soft answers.* Scenario techniques are usually qualitative, based on reasoning and intuitive pattern recognition, although thorough analysis is often part of the process. The results are often presented in qualitative terms that fit poorly with traditional numbers-oriented cultures.
- *Time consuming.* Another reason why top managers are so rarely involved in scenario projects is that workshop-based methods are time consuming in terms of the number of hours and days the participants need to spend to get thorough

results. To avoid that, we often recommend designs where important internal stakeholders are involved in the critical moments, but where the project group consists of selected members with relevant backgrounds and the right mindset and, not least, more time available.

What constitutes a good scenario?

This book is about scenario planning: we are concerned with scenarios in the context of strategic planning. But how do we identify good scenarios in that context?

There are in short seven criteria for a good scenario set for strategy purposes:

- *Decision-making power.* Each scenario in the set, and the set as a whole, must provide insights useful for the question being considered. Most generic industry or general scenario sets lack this power and need to be complemented for decision purposes.
- *Plausibility.* The developed scenarios must fall within the limits of what future events that are realistically possible.
- *Alternatives.* Each scenario should be at least to some extent probable, although it is not necessary to define the probabilities explicitly. The ideal is that the scenarios are all more or less equally probable, so that the widest possible range of uncertainty is covered by the scenario set. If for instance only one of three or four scenarios is probable, you only have one scenario in reality.
- *Consistency.* Each scenario must be internally consistent. Without internal consistency the scenarios will not be credible. The logic of the scenario is critical.
- *Differentiation.* The scenarios should be structurally or qualitatively different. Thus it is not enough for them to be different in terms of magnitude, and therefore only variations of a base scenario.
- *Memorability.* The scenarios should be easy to remember and to differentiate, even after a presentation. Therefore it is advisable to reduce the number to between three and five, although in theory we could remember and differentiate up to seven or eight scenarios. Vivid scenario names help.
- *Challenge.* The final criterion is that scenarios really challenge the organization's received wisdom about the future.

DEVELOPING SCENARIOS

Scenarios can be developed in many different ways and be used for a range of and purposes.

There are, basically, three major types of scenarios – trend-based, contrasted and normative scenarios – linked to probable, possible and desired/undesired futures. Business decisions can be framed and justified through the use of trend-based scenarios (the most probable type in the future business or decision context) and normative scenarios (visions or challenging scenarios). With contrasted sets of scenarios, the decision context can be explored, existing concepts and other factors be evaluated, and better decisions be made. Sets of contrasted scenarios are usually what we talk about when we discuss scenario planning, and it is this type of scenario that is considered in this book.

Ways to develop scenarios

There are several different ways of conducting a scenario process. The simplest is the expert model, in which one person or a small group does the work (Table 2.3).

Table 2.3. Three models for carrying out a scenario project

	Expert model	Participation model	Organization model
The planner works	Alone	With a group in the organization	In training/ instructing the organization
Control	The planner controls the process	The planner takes part in and leads the process	The planner stays outside the process
The result	Is presented by the planner	Is owned and presented by the group	Is owned by the organization
Relationship	The planner completes the assignment	The planner maintains a relationship with the group	The planner passes responsibility to the group

In the participation model, the expert acts as project leader together with a group of people from the organization. The group then owns the result. The expert could come either from inside the organization or from outside. It is often desirable to have external facilitators, and even workshop members, at some stages in the scenario process in order to bring external perspectives into the process.

In the organization model, the expert trains a group of people in the organization, who then carry out the work. The result will be owned completely by the organization or the group within it that did the work.

Some form of participation model, with a series of seminars and dialogues with key persons, is often to be preferred.

A BRIEF HISTORY OF SCENARIO PLANNING

Fundamentally, as neurologist David Ingvar used to point out, *Homo sapiens* is a scenario-writing animal. None the less, the modern development of scenario writing only began at a late stage in human history.

The roots of scenario planning

In brief we could say that scenario planning in the shape we meet it in businesses around the world has two primary roots. The first is futurism, where scenario analysis early became an important method and scenarios an effective presentation format. The second is strategy, where strategists and managers since the 1970s have searched for new and more relevant tools to work with complex issues. While the futurists used scenarios as a mean to analyse, debate and communicate the 'big issues', the strategists were interested in them as a powerful planning instrument. The questions were not primarily 'what might happen?', but 'what should we do?'

A third root on the tree of scenario planning emerged in the 1990s, growing from the tradition of organizational development and learning. In the spirit of scholars and authors like Peter Senge (author of *The Fifth Discipline*) organizational learning, shared visions and world views, and collectively developed strategies became primary issues. Scenario workshop techniques were then found to be excellent formats for this work.

Both futurism and strategy are young, immature disciplines, and multi-disciplinary by nature. They have emerged over the last 40 years as a response to the more complex global issues and organizations. Strategic planning developed during the 1960s in the work of scholars like Chandler, Ansoff and Lawrence and Lorsch, and has evolved into a number of schools and traditions over the years. From the early beginnings, coping with uncertainty has been considered 'the essence of the administrative process', as J. D. Thompson put it.

Futurism

The field of futurism dates back to the ancient prophets, as well as to visionaries and artists like Thomas More (*Utopia*, 1516), Francis Bacon (*The New Atlantis*, 1626) and Edward Bellamy (*Looking Backwards*, 1888). In its more modern form it goes back to the 1940s and 1950s, when people like Bertrand de Jouvenel, Robert Jungk and Herman Kahn developed methodologies and perspectives for dealing with the future. The European school, represented by Jouvenel and Jungk, and later by institutes like the Copenhagen Institute for Future Studies and the Swedish Secretariat for Future Studies, was more qualitatively and policy oriented than the American representatives. The focus was more on possible and desired futures than probable ones. During the golden years of the 1970s a number of institutions and organizations promoting futures studies were born. It became an academic discipline with master's degrees, and associations such as the World Future Society and World Future Studies Federation were founded. Future studies were often comprehensive and extensive, dealing with the big issues like global natural resources, population growth, North–South conflict and *The Next 200 Years* (the title of Herman Kahn's 1978 book). The most famous production from that time is probably the Club of Rome's *Limits to Growth* (1972). A number of independent thinkers also presented bestsellers, like Alvin Toffler's *Future Shock* (1973) and Daniel Bell's *The Post-Industrial Society* (1976).

During the 1980s' planning crises, the field of futurism shifted from extensive studies towards pop-futurism. Authors like John Naisbitt (*Megatrends*) and later Faith Popcorn became the new futurist stars. Since around 1990, futurism has had something of a renaissance. Foresight projects have been taken up as policy instruments by governmental bodies and scenario activities have almost become part of the everyday toolbox. At the same time a flood of books has come onto the market, basically highlighting the new technologies, new paradigms and the new economy. Manuel Castell's seminal work on *The Network Society* was the most ambitious of them all, and was compared with Karl Marx's work of the industrial age.

Strategy

Strategy has been defined in a number of ways. The root is the Greek word *strategos*, meaning 'a general'. The Greek word *stratego* means to 'plan the destruction of one's enemies through effective use of resources' (Bracker 1980), or the art of a general.

James Brian Quinn once defined strategy more precisely as

> the pattern or plan that integrates an organization's major goals, policies, and actions into a cohesive whole. A well-formulated strategy helps to marshal and allocate an organization's resources into a unique and viable posture based on its relative internal competences and shortcomings, anticipated changes in the environment, and contingent moves by intelligent opponents.
>
> (Quinn 1995: 12)

But what does that mean in practice? Are good strategies really planned, or do they emerge (Mintzberg 1994)? Is it possible to identify a good strategy beforehand, or can we only do so in retrospect? Although strategy as a discipline has been around for almost 40 years the field of strategic management is characterized, today more than ever, by contrasting and competing paradigms (Hamel and Heene 1994). There is still no consensus in the strategy field around basic questions such as 'what is a theory of strategic management about?' or 'what should a theory of strategic management be about?'

As we have already noted, the field of strategy research in management dates back to the early works of scholars such as Chandler, Ansoff, Lawrence and Lorch, and Thompson and Andrews.[14] The concept of strategy was either to design an optimal strategy, or to formulate a strategic plan. During the 1970s strategy emerged as an academic discipline with its own journals and societies like the Strategic Management Society (founded 1982), where scholars and practitioners exchange experiences.

During the 1980s, a new wave swept strategic management research. Triggered by the work of Miles and Snow (1978) and Porter (1980; 1985), strategic content research flourished, emphasizing the characteristics of successful strategies rather than how they are formed. In the 1990s another revolution took place, shifting the focus from the content of strategy to the strategic decision-making process, hyper-competition and high-velocity environments, organizational capabilities and evolutionary aspects of strategy.[15]

During the 1990s, more companies and industries were faced with rapid and continuous change. A number of studies have focused on firms operating in that kind of highly unstable, uncertain and hostile environment, finding that such an environment requires innovative differentiation strategies combined with organic, specialized and integrated organizations.[16]

Consequently, in the context of highly turbulent environments strategy tends to be defined more as a posture or a combination of activities in order to achieve competitive advantage than as a plan to destroy the enemy. [17] Lengnick-Hall and Wolf (1999) identified three major schools of the 1990s. The first school is based on capability logic, emphasizing the need for superior resources. The second makes use of guerrilla logic, focusing on the need for speed. The third rests on complexity logic, which emphasizes the need for a deeper understanding of the underlying forces and attractors in the business environment. The scenario planning perspective has the ability to integrate all of these.

Scenario planning

Let us return to the field of scenario planning. Most authors attribute the modern scenario tradition to Herman Kahn and the RAND Corporation in the 1950s. Kahn developed a technique he called a 'future-now' thinking. He adopted the term 'scenario' when Hollywood decreed the term outdated and switched to the label 'screenplay'. The scenarios he developed were part of military strategy research conducted at RAND for the US Government. Later Kahn expanded the scenario scope to other areas after he founded the Hudson Institute in the mid-1960s. In a number of studies and books he actively promoted the idea of 'thinking the unthinkable'.

In the 1970s scenario planning spread outside the RAND and Hudson Institute. Companies like Royal Dutch/Shell and consultants such as SRI International and Batelle adopted scenarios as part of their strategy repertoire, and scenario planning thus became more closely related to strategy. Shell is also generally credited as the first company to use scenarios widely as a strategy tool in the corporate setting. Pierre Wack, Arie de Gues and Kees van der Heijden are some of the famous scenario masters from that time. As early as 1967, Pierre Wack and Ted Newland had suggested that thinking six years ahead was not enough and started to plan for the year 2000. When the Yom Kippur war broke out Shell was prepared. The ability to foresee possible futures and to act quickly has been credited as the primary reason behind the company's success during recent years (van der Heijden 1996).

Scenario thinking diffused into businesses as Stanford Research Institute began offering them long-range planning and bodies such as the Hudson Institute began to seek corporate sponsors for their projects. Shell's success with the scenario planning approach also encouraged the majority of the Fortune 1000 companies to adopt scenarios in one way or another during the 1970s.

During the 1970s a number of national bodies were funded to study the future. Many of them took up scenario planning as a central futures exploration tool, among them the Swedish Secretariat for Future Studies.

The scenario planning era during the 1970s was short lived however. The recession following the oil crises in the mid and late 1970s forced corporations to cut corporate staff. Oversimplified scenarios came in for criticism, often justifiably. This, along with long-standing habits of rigid long-term planning, and a failure to distinguish scenarios from forecasts, led corporations to return to more traditional ways of planning.

The planning crises of the 1980s, however, led to renewed interest in how planning happens, leading many futures consultancy firms to develop scenario planning methodologies. The turbulence of the 1990s and the renewed interest in managing uncertainty through scenario thinking and planning have caused all major management consultancies to develop their own scenario methodologies. Today, scenarios still play a major role at Shell and, although Shell is often considered the corporate champion of scenarios, turbulence scenario planning has become a more or less standard tool in most companies and consultancy firms' toolboxes over the last decade or so.

TAIDA™: A FRAMEWORK FOR THINKING OF THE FUTURE

As we already have seen, the brain basically functions as a scenario generating organ. In that sense it constantly scans the environments, tries to make sense of what it perceives, identifies alternative future developments, alternative goals and actions, decides what to do – and makes sure that necessary steps are taken.

Transformed into a scenario planning framework, we could talk about the brain's 'TAIDA process': Tracking, Analysing, Imaging, Deciding and Acting. TAIDA is also the name of the framework we have developed and used for more than ten years in hundreds of scenario planning projects for public and private businesses and organizations. In short TAIDA stands for:

- *Tracking:* we trace changes and signs of threats and opportunities.
- *Analysing:* we analyse consequences and generate scenarios.
- *Imaging:* we identify possibilities and generate visions of what is desired.
- *Deciding:* we weigh up the information, identify choices and strategies.
- *Acting:* we set up short-term goals, take the first steps and follow up our actions.

If you compare the TAIDA framework with what we described in Chapter 1 as key organizational capabilities (namely to quickly observe, orient, decide and act), you can see that it is actually the same framework. Tracking is about 'observing' changes. Analysing and Imaging are about 'orienting'. Imaging and Deciding are about 'deciding' and Acting, naturally, is about 'acting'.

In Chapter 3 we will describe more extensively how that framework could be put into practice. But let us first take a look at the more philosophical argument for its logic.

Tracking: having your eyes and ears open

All living beings must be aware of the dangers in their immediate surroundings. That is as true of the antelope on the savannah as for the teenager in the back streets of the Bronx. A temporary lapse of attention can mean the end.

What applies to individuals, whether people or animals, also applies to organizations, companies and nations. Just as the antelope must continually prick up its ears and sniff the air to detect the sound or smell of approaching danger in time, the organization must listen to small, perhaps unclear signals from its surroundings. And like the antelope, the organization must learn to seek out the right signals, namely those that reveal danger ahead.

But there are also other signals that are vital to antelopes, people and organizations: those that reveal which way to go to find green pastures. These signals are often difficult to detect. Often there are no signs in our immediate surroundings saying the grass is greener 20 kilometres to the west. The ground shows no evidence of it. In such situations it is necessary to find other signals that can indicate which direction to take.

The danger lies in our inability to discover the unexpected, our tendency to look where the light is shining.

Analysing: what is really happening?

When you are on the track of something interesting, when you have seen that a pattern is changing in a particular direction, the questions that follow are often: What will happen if it carries on like this? What will the consequence be for us – and for others? What connections are there between the changes in this and other fields?

If tracking is about getting on the track of changes, discovering patterns, trends, threats and opportunities, analysing is about discovering future consequences of changes in the present, and the interplay between trends and tendencies. Analysis goes a stage further than what we called tracking. It aims at tackling questions such as: What is happening in what seems to be happening? Which are lasting tendencies and which fleeting ripples on the surface?

But the analysis can also aim at delving deeper into creative and intuitively produced scenarios, models and visions. The questions are then, for example: What are the necessary conditions for this to become reality? How tenable is this model? What are its weak points? What are its strengths?

Imaging: bringing your dreams to life

The purpose of tracking is to trace changes and make contact with them. The purpose of analysing is to get an in-depth understanding of the changes and the interplay that can be observed, and from that try to find patterns and connections. The purpose of imaging is more airy. Here it is a matter of approaching changes and courses of events more intuitively, to create not only an intellectual understanding but also an emotional meaning. This is what happens when we put life into alternative futures. Creating images in the mind enables us to develop an emotional relationship to the alternative futures we are faced with. We can discover our own intentions, our own will and our own relationships to them, and in that way acquire a good foundation for strategic choices.

Only the person who really wants to create something succeeds. That is well known in sports psychology. The key to success in sport, of course, is action. To reach the top you must train and train and train, come rain or shine. But to train hard, you must really want to reach the top. And the will is often bound up with a conception of meaning. Training is worthwhile because I have prospects of succeeding. I know I can achieve the results I want, such as the speed needed to win a gold medal in an international tournament.

Common to most great athletes is that they repeatedly bring their victories to life. When Bob Beaman set his 'unbeatable' world long-jump record in the Mexico Olympics of 1968, we know the external conditions were good. The air was thin at that high altitude and he had a slight following wind. But what is less well known is that he had already made the jump. Therefore he knew he could do it. He had already jumped in his mind.

Deciding: selecting and rejecting

When you make your own personal decisions, take part in decisions at meetings, or are faced with choosing the direction to take – either in your work situation or on your own behalf – you do it on more or less good grounds, but with a fairly clear idea of what you want to achieve. More often than not you have a goal before your eyes that you want to see realized. You want a result that is clear to your inner vision.

Decision lies along the road between vision and action. Choosing a direction, sometimes irrevocably, is a moment of truth. Therefore some decisions can be difficult to take, not least a decision to make a move and leave something behind you.

Visions and decisions are mental processes that take place in a social and professional context. The ways and methods of producing visions are varied and less developed than the decision procedure itself, which is formalized and well known. The vision expresses what is desired and worth striving for. The decision process is concrete; it evaluates and tests.

The ability to take decisions and make the connection with concrete action separates the entrepreneur from the dreamer. The dreamer can be skilful in assessing what is practicable, seeing what should be done and what could be done. But he falls short when it comes to action. The extremely intuitive and possibility-oriented person often has difficulty in making decisions. He wants a more secure foundation on which to base them. There are so many possibilities. If we wait a while longer there'll be even more . . .

Acting: presence and learning

Learning can be said to be mastering the art of integrating new information into old knowledge, while having a clear purpose. For your organization to learn something, it must consist of individuals who are able to take in signals from the outside world and the inside world; people who work and act, with their work aimed at producing results. Doing and acting are therefore central skills in this learning process, just as purpose and visions are, of course.

Doing and acting are both operative skills that are decisive for the success and survival of an organization. Naturally, things are done and action taken in all organizations, but with the most varying results. The organization will be most efficient, and probably most successful, if each member of the staff has learnt to foresee and act and be a step ahead, and thus does not need to devote time and energy to countering emergency situations.

For the activities to have the penetration intended, keep their focus and be as durable as planned, it is extraordinarily important for the organization's action to be centred on the vision. This 'centred' action is one of the key factors for efficiency and success that can be affected and learnt by both staff and the organization as a whole. It is like Tai Chi, where you have to fill yourself with all the necessary concentration for the purpose of carrying out movements as precisely as possible with the least possible expenditure of energy, or like the tennis player whose action is centred on playing for each particular point and not the final result. He or she reads the opponent's movement pattern and can therefore see in advance where the ball will land. This makes it possible to get into the right position in good time to concentrate on the return shot. But to act in that way there must be a vision – of balance and perfection in Tai Chi, and of the winning shot and the notion of winning the match for the tennis player. For you and me it is a matter of keeping the vision alive and ignoring what is irrelevant, but also of learning to rely on what we intuitively perceive and doing what is essential.

SCENARIO PLANNING AND LEADERSHIP

Where do scenario planning and futures thinking enter into leadership and management systems? Let us conclude this introduction by putting scenario planning into a broader context.

We can take as our starting point a picture of the company as a system with two subsystems, each with partly different purposes and goals. The system on the right in Figure 2.8 is oriented towards development and learning, capturing changes in the outside world, new needs and challenges and formulating replies to them. The currency in this system is qualitative, a matter of inclination, involvement and energy. The system on the left is oriented towards production, efficiency and results. The currency is quantitative. The two systems could be likened to the two halves of the organization's brain. In this picture, leadership has three dimensions:

- *Creative:* oriented towards development and renewal. The guiding principle is process and vision control.
- *Efficient:* oriented towards production and results. The guiding principle is management of objectives
- *Integrating:* concerned with the right and left sides of the brain together. This has three aspects:
    - Planning, that is, introducing structures into the creative right half of the brain and forming ideas and visions into concrete goals and plans.
    - Decision making, which is concerned with managing conflicts, knowing when a lot of different ideas are wanted and when a plan should be followed.
    - Support, concerned with putting desire and involvement into the everyday working of the left half of the brain.

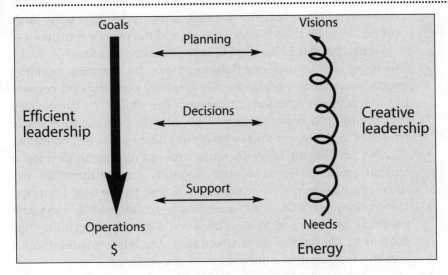

Figure 2.8. The two 'brain-halves' of the organization

With this picture it is clear that scenario planning is a leadership instrument primarily for the right side of the brain and for integration between the left and right halves. When we get into the question of implementing the strategies that have grown out of scenario planning, we start getting deeper into the left half of the brain.

PARADOXES IN SCENARIO PLANNING

It is clear from the description above that scenario planning is not a very well-defined field. Rather, it is a multiplicity of perspectives and methods that could be used in various contexts, in different ways and for various purposes. Consequently, the field of scenario planning is crowded with contradictions and paradoxes that have to be dealt with before and during a scenario planning activity. As a summary of this introductory chapter we will raise just a few of them.

- *Planning and learning.* What is the main purpose of the activity?
- *Multiplicity and simplification.* Rich and complex scenario sets are useful if you want to explore alternatives or create preparedness for the future, but do not provide the simplicity and security that most managers like best.
- *Complexity and bandwidth limitation.* A set of scenarios must be complex enough to cover the most relevant dimensions of external

uncertainty. However, the mental capacity to deal with large numbers of scenarios is very limited, and the practical number of scenarios that could be used is between three and five.

- *Divergent and convergent thinking.* Powerful scenario building needs both divergent (alternative, creative) thinking and convergent (analytical) thinking. However, the ability to think both divergently and convergently is not always present in a single person. The divergent and convergent phases must be separated.
- *Process and analysis.* A scenario process aiming to develop a shared understanding of the decision environment or the future prospects does not necessarily lead to the best analysis.
- *Uncertainty creation and uncertainty management.* Scenario methods can be used to identify ways to create uncertainty (for others) in the business environment, but also to understand and manage central dimensions of uncertainty.
- *Innovation and evaluation.* Scenario planning designed for innovation purposes are necessarily different from processes aiming to evaluate existing concepts, strategies and the like.
- *Long term and short term.* In the short term, trend-based scenarios are often enough since most changes have already happened. But in the long term uncertainties and discontinuities are more critical. When the focus is on action, a short-term view is appropriate. Long-term perspectives are still needed, however, to provide a relevant contextual framing for the short-term decisions.
- *Forecasting and back-casting.* Scenarios can be developed through either a present-to-future perspective or through a retrospective approach using back-casting.
- *Thinkers and decision makers.* How much should line managers and other decision makers be involved in the process? Involving line managers and other decision makers carries the risk that office politics may complicate the process, but makes it more likely that the decisions will be implemented.
- *Internal perspectives or involvement of outsiders (consultants, experts, clients).* Scenario processes can be undertaken without the involvement of outsiders. Outsiders may provide useful perspectives, but could also cause the discussion to become less open.
- *Closed versus open-ended.* Scenarios may be used with a specific decision in mind, but may also be more open-ended explorative processes.

- *Research-based and intuitive.* Scenario building is fundamentally an intuitive and creative process. However, it must be based on thorough research into present and past conditions and future developments and trends.
- *Intellectual and emotional.* Scenario planning is an intellectual process, since it deals with what might happen. However, in order to influence decisions, the thinking must also touch the heart. Decision makers must be engaged – whether worried or enthusiastic – by the scenarios, and thus they must also be emotional.
- *Advocacy and dialogue.* An open dialogue is needed to develop good scenarios. However, powerful advocacy for certain scenarios can energize the process and sharpen the logic and arguments, as long as the advocacy does not go to extremes.
- *Scepticism and expertise.* Expertise is always needed in a scenario process, but is not enough by itself. A well-grounded scepticism that challenges preconceptions and prejudices is also needed.
- *Quantitative and qualitative.* Scenarios are essentially imaginative constructs. But in order to get credibility they often need to be grounded in quantitatively based arguments, and expressed in some quantitative ways.
- *Probability and plausibility.* Should the scenarios emphasize the probable futures (as is necessary for short-term decisions) or plausible longer-term futures, or both?

WHEN CAN SCENARIO TECHNIQUES BE USED?

It is time to summarize some of the conclusions so far. Let us start with the questions of when scenario techniques could be used.

In the planning cycle from contextual analysis (tracking) to implementation (action), scenario techniques can be used at several stages (Figure 2.9). Scenario techniques are powerful tools to identify contextual challenges and opportunities. Both trend-based scenarios and contrasted, alternative scenarios could be used as a basis for generating and selecting strategic issues. We will later describe in more detail how this can be done. The selected issues and identified consequences of the contextual changes could be used to generate strategic options. Scenarios could also be used directly for that purpose. The construction of composite strategies from strategic options cannot be based directly on scenarios, but scenarios and scenario-based techniques could be used to select and evaluate new or existing strategies.

The same is true for the development of visions. It is fundamental to strategic management that visions, goals and resources and competences are in line with the business environment. Scenario techniques can be useful in developing a strategic vision that creates stretch, and thus the energy necessary to keep the organization going.

Strategy implementation is just as important as strategy development (if not more so). Without a good implementation strategy and effective implementation, strategy development will be nothing more than an intellectual exercise. Practical implementation does not make much use of scenarios, although scenarios and visions can function as guidelines. But in the development of the implementation strategy in terms of organizational needs, operations design and so on, scenario techniques are as useful as in the development of corporate or business strategies. Finally, scenarios can be useful in the evaluation of the company's progress and course of action. 'Are we heading in the right direction, given the most probable business context scenarios and their alternatives?' is a question that should be asked more frequently in many organizations.

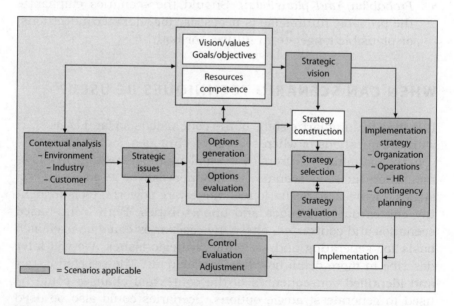

Figure 2.9. Different planning situations where scenarios are useful

Scenario Planning in Practice

In the previous chapters we have given an overview of what scenario planning is all about, why it is needed and the principles of scenario and strategic thinking. Now it is time to show how to make use of scenario planning as a powerful tool in strategic planning processes. We will go all the way from considering how to determine focal questions and project design, through scenarios and visions, to ways of developing strategies that can be put into action.

TAIDA™: THE METHOD FOR SCENARIO PLANNING

In Chapter 2 we introduced TAIDA from a philosophical angle. TAIDA™ is a well-tried model for scenario planning. Hundreds of scenario projects have been carried out on the basis of the model in the past decade. In some cases they have been projects of an expert character, but most often they have been more interactive processes in which a large part of the work has been done in workshops. In this chapter we will show and exemplify how the model can be used as a framework for scenario planning processes.

First a short reminder of the five steps of TAIDA:

- *Tracking.* The first step in the TAIDA process is tracking. The main purpose of this step is to trace and describe changes in the surrounding world that may have an impact on the focal question.
- *Analysing.* With the tracking done, the next step is to analyse changes and generate scenarios.
- *Imaging.* After gathering insights about plausible futures, it is time to create images of what is desired: visions.
- *Deciding.* In this phase of the process we identify development areas and strategies to meet threats and achieve visions and goals.
- *Acting.* Plans in themselves rarely give results. Acting is about taking action and following up. We will show how scenario planning can be followed up.

| Tracking | Analysing | Imaging | Deciding | Acting |

Figure 3.1. Overview of the TAIDA process

But before we get any deeper into the five steps of the TAIDA model we will take a look at the preparations for a scenario project.

PREPARATIONS

The starting phase of a project is extremely important. That is not news and we all know it. All the same we are often so exited about getting started that we do not stop to analyse the purpose of the project. Sometimes we do not even define the specific question that is most important to solve. This will often lead to disaster, as we all know. Unfortunately, it is easy to overlook a woolly purpose in a scenario planning project as it is all about looking into the future, a future that seems vague. The preparations are however crucial. The question can become so complex and involve so much information that it is easy to drown in floods of irrelevant information that effectively hinder a good overview.

The purpose of the scenario planning process

It is advisable to begin by focusing on the reasons for starting a process. As we have already seen, scenario planning can have different purposes. Is it most important to create the prerequisites for change in the organization, or to find the right track and go into action? Is the focus on finding new business or improving old? The ways scenario planning processes are designed, as well as the outcomes of the processes, are essentially dependent on the combination of purpose and focus (see Figure 2.3 in Chapter 2).

Risk consciousness/need for renewal

This kind of scenario planning emphasizes the prerequisites for change and focuses on old business. Its original aim was to increase preparedness for unexpected courses of events. Another important function is to increase insight into the need for renewal, often at a time when the new direction is difficult or impossible to foresee. Its main purpose is to create scenarios that can be used as eye-openers.

Example

A couple of years ago some colleagues of ours carried out a scenario process for the Energy Ministry in Colombia. They raised questions about the future supply of and demand for energy in the region. They realized that the question was complex, as it dealt with anything from environmental changes to standards of living and the ongoing civil war. The intention was that the scenarios should increase risk awareness as well as leading to a consensus on the need for renewal. They decided on a relatively broad scenario process in order to map alternative futures for the energy sector of Colombia. Interested parties from ministry to producers met for a number of seminars over a period of more than a year. They ended up with a set of four alternative future scenarios that would each have a great impact on future energy supply and demand. The process was facilitated by three European scenario planners.

New thinking/paradigm shift

Identifying the prerequisite for change is the essential point here too, though the focus is on new business. The reason for starting the process is often an insight among some people that changes in the surrounding world will offer prospects for new kinds of solutions or even a new paradigm. The direction to take in the future, however, is not obvious. The main purpose is to create and evaluate alternative strategies or solutions that have chances of success in a new and still unknown world.

Example

A region situated some hundred miles north of Stockholm, Sweden, had seen a small but increasing downturn in population, together with reduced employment in the heavy industries that had dominated the region for more than a century. There was an insight among regional leaders that something had to be done to make the region more competitive. When we started the project we were in the middle of the new economic boom and some people claimed that there was a para-digm shift coming. Others, mainly those who were deeply involved in the traditional industries, were equally convinced that heavy industry would dominate even in the future. What alternative societies might develop and what kind of actions could be helpful in respective scenar-ios? An essential purpose of the scenario process was to broaden insights into possible future changes within the society. The strategies that came out of the project had to be shared by politicians and plan-ners as well as by industrialists and citizens. The process stretched over more than a year and involved around 80 people from all parts of the region. The scenarios and strategies that were developed are now being used as the basis of a dialogue with people in the society of the region.

Business development/concept development

Action as well as new business is central in this kind of scenario planning. The reason for starting the process could be either a realization that the old products or services will not be successful in a changing world, or an intention to find development areas for new technology. The main purpose is to create and evaluate alter-native business concepts or products that are likely prosper in a future world.

Example

A small company had developed a breakthrough interface between computers and operators. They saw many possible applications but the costs and time needed to develop each product were so high that they had to understand the future logic of the market many years before launching time. What kind of applications would the market be interested in and at what price? When would it be possible to produce the actual goods at a price that the market would be willing to pay? Our task was to help them find an effective strategy that would enable them to find the right timing of product development to meet future market demands appropriately. We carried out the project over a period of six days with a team of three scenario planners and three people from the company. The result was that they came up with a strategic plan that was fully owned by the management and praised by the major investors.

Strategy development/organizational development

Action is central here too, but in combination with a focus on old business. Major improvements are needed from the perspective of changes in the outer or inner world. The main purpose is to raise the readiness for change and also to find the best strategies for the future. The process often provides an insight into major changes in a futures perspective.

Example

Swedish municipalities have seen huge changes in demands from their citizens at the same time as budgets had to be cut. The Association of Swedish Local Authorities realized that they would face new challenges in the coming years. They decided on a qualitative scenario process as a complement to the traditional prognosis. Early on, they realized that it was important that the scenario analysis was owned by the municipalities, and they decided to invite 100 people from all over Sweden. The participants were politicians of all persuasions and civil servants: young and old, men and women. The process stretched over a year and included six two-day seminars. The process followed TAIDA and was led by an internal project group together with four professional scenario planners who acted as facilitators as well as experts. The broad process inspired participants to start future-oriented projects back home. The result of the project was a better understanding of how people in Sweden would live in the year 2015 and how that would challenge the municipalities.

The examples show that different purposes put different demands on the scenario planning process. In some cases it is fully possible to work with a small and dedicated task force; in other cases it is necessary to involve lots of people in the process. The format of the focal question also has an impact on the choice of methodology.

TASK AND PREREQUISITES

Identifying the system that is to be analysed

It is quite possible to look at the future of the organization as a whole. This can be a productive approach, especially if the operation is fairly homogenous and acts in markets that are very similar. On the other hand, if the organization is a conglomerate of disparate operations, the picture of the environmental changes and the scenarios could be too generalized and will give little or no guidance. Sometimes, therefore, it is better to take a deeper look at the specific operations that are particularly exposed to a complex environment characterized by rapid change. Very often though, a broad view of the future can help to find the operations where it is worth making a deeper analysis. A deeper look into a specific system at a lower organizational level will also give insights that are applicable on a higher level. You can follow the line of reasoning that normally takes place in the three examples below.

If the purpose is, for example, to draw up a competence-provision plan for a daily newspaper company, it would be appropriate to look at the company's business strategies and perceptions of the future market. These may then be seen to be unclear and the Human Resources Department may be forced to step in and, in consultation with other departments, produce images of the future market that can be the basis for discussion about the consequences for competence needs and other aspects. Thus in this case, the scenarios should be concentrated on the future of the market for daily papers, despite the fact that the task is to draw up a competence-provision plan.

If the purpose is for a pharmaceutical company to draw up strategies for future action in a changed market, the market for pharmaceutical products is a suitable system to study. The questions to work on are, for example: What can conceivably affect the market in the future? What are the major factors making for change? And how are they being changed? Are there other possible developments? The visions then produced should deal with the company's own action on the market and be matched by different possible market-development patterns.

A medical organization that wants to change the role of doctors and raise their status must acquire an understanding of the kind of medical-care system their role should be related to. To work on images of the doctor's role in the future, it is first necessary to work on scenarios of future medical care.

Defining the focal questions

The answer you get is no better than the question you ask. A woolly question will get a woolly answer. A specific question will produce more specific answers.

In a project for the R&D department of a global enterprise our task was to find strategies for the future. R&D departments are among the most interesting parts of organizations to do scenario planning for. They generally need to work with a horizon of anything from 2 to 20 years: two years if they are looking at the product development phase in mature product-segments, but 20 years when it comes to building knowledge for future research and development. When we started to define the question about strategies, it appeared that the R&D department in fact wanted answers to two different questions. Their first concern was to find out what kinds of competence they would need to develop tomorrow's products. Their second was to focus on how to attract, keep and develop competence in the organization. We soon found out that the driving forces and trends that had an impact on the two different focuses were very different. The result was that we had to identify the changes in the environment from two different starting points. The set of trends that had the highest impact on the respective questions were by no means the same. The two questions, even though they concerned competence of the same R&D department, followed two different logics.

Time horizon

The time horizon is as essential as the focal question. If we look just a few years ahead, there will probably be very little difference. If on the other hand we look 20 years ahead much may have changed. The uncertainty is huge, however, perhaps too huge to find answers that can give any guidance for the organization. The time horizon for scenarios must be short enough to create scenarios that are probable, but long enough for us to imagine that important changes with an impact on the future business can take place.

Defining the past and the present

Although scenario planning processes concern the future, it is important to have a clear picture of the present and the past. What is the history of the organization and how has it developed up to now? How has the competitive landscape developed and what have been the triggers for change? Which have been the main indicators of changes in the landscape so far?

You might object that the future landscape is extremely uncertain and that there are many new threats and possibilities. But there are a lot of driving forces in the surrounding world that remain the same. The logic of the arena is still there and even if you consider that your organization is very future-oriented, it is most probable that the changes are fairly slow and that you have competitors who are forerunners as well as followers. An insight into how they think can help you in your planning process.

Another parameter concerns the inner life of your organization. What is the attitude to the environment around the organization and future issues. There are huge differences in the best way to conduct a scenario planning process in a fairly new IT business compared with one for a company that has been successful for years and years in a market with no sign of big changes.

All these aspects have a great impact on people's attitudes, openness to change, risk awareness and willingness to try new approaches. This will of course affect the way the process is structured.

History and the current situation: draw a current-situation map and clarify underlying conditions

When the issue has been formulated, you have to obtain an overall picture of the current situation and history, that is, the underlying conditions. The current-situation map should cover both 'the players' and the system you, as a group of players, want to analyse. You have to clarify the underlying conditions for the scenario analysis as well as for visions and strategies: in other words, all the phases of TAIDA.

If we go back to the newspaper company, the work at this stage is to clarify the current situation and history not only of its own paper but also of the daily press industry, which is what the scenario analysis will primarily concentrate on. The questions will be: What does the industry look like today? What part do we play in it? What difference do newspapers make? Who loves us? Who wants change? What do we say about ourselves? What is our competence provision like today? What is the worst that can happen? What are the issues in the industry today?

History and driving forces are often missed out in strategic analyses, and it is then easy for the work to become a 'technical' matter.

Another important point is to be clear about the aim of the process. The way to structure the process and the level of involvement in the organization depend on the purpose. If the main task is to come up with better overall strategies for the organization, it is often enough to bring together an open-minded group with good insights, thinking abilities and capacities for comprehensive thinking. On the other hand, if it is more important to increase awareness of prospective changes that may alter the future competitive landscape, it is important to broaden the process and involve as many people as possible. This decision implies different points of attack to the scenario process.

TRACKING

With a clear purpose, a distinct focal question with a specified time horizon, and a good map of the present and the past, it is time to start looking at the future. We call this 'tracking', as it is a matter of tracking changes in the environment that may have an impact on the focal question.

Tracking is about finding trends, drivers and uncertainties that need to be considered in the work, since they influence the future of the 'question'. Many companies have a business intelligence function, but they normally focus on the present and devote most energy to the competitive landscape within their own line of business. Of course there are organizations that regularly track and analyse trends in the surrounding world, but in our experience they are rather rare. For this reason we start by pointing out methods and tools that can be used by those who have relatively little experience. In the appendix we give an overview of more advanced methods.

Viewpoint: outside–in

The normal perspective for most organizations is from inside to out. They start by looking at their own organization and then at customers, competitors, structures and technology within their own arena. It is quite rare for them to look more deeply into the driving forces behind the changes on the arena. This approach works as long as its rather narrow outlook is appropriate. For example, it can be adequate if you are going to plan market activities for the next few years in a stable environment. On the other hand, if the focus is on long-term product development in a complex and rapidly changing environment, this perspective is inadequate. The inside–out perspective makes it difficult to predict changes in the marketplace that have not already become evident. To anticipate these changes it is necessary to start by looking at the driving forces that may have an impact on what happens in the arena affecting the business of the organization (Figure 3.2).

Long-term developments in the arena very largely depend on driving forces in the surrounding world. Therefore the natural starting point for tracking is trends in the surrounding world.

What is a trend?

What we mean by a trend is something that represents a deeper change, not a fad. If we make an analogy with meteorology, trends would be climate changes rather than variations in the weather.

When people talk of the future, they normally talk in terms of what they think will happen. These thoughts are very seldom relevant because they tend to be projections of either what people

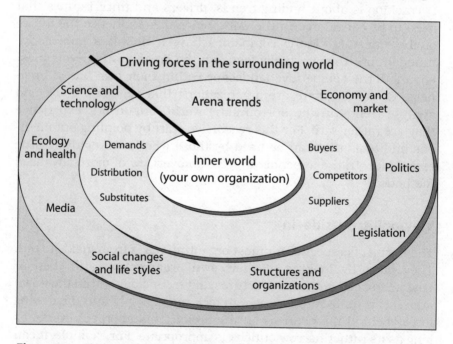

Figure 3.2. The outside–in perspective of scenario planning

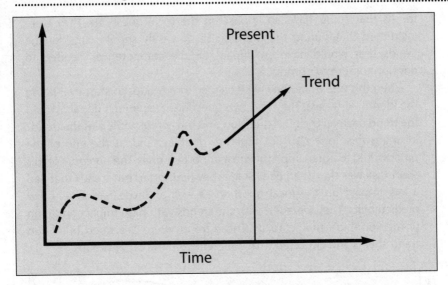

Figure 3.3. Trends are based on observed changes in the present

would like to see (daydreams or visions) or what they are afraid of (nightmares or threats). When we work with trends, we start in the present and try to look at changes that can be observed: there has already been a change for some time in a certain direction.

How to identify trends

One reason why many organizations do not try to look deeper into future is that it seems so complicated as to be for professional futurists only. If you look at some of the methods that we introduce in the appendix you might be deterred from starting. Normally though, it is more productive to take a simpler route in order to get started. The more advanced methods can then be used as a complement when it comes to looking at specific trends that needs deeper analysis.

Example

In the project concerning the R&D department we mentioned earlier, the purpose was to develop and prioritize strategies. We had not too much time for tracking of trends. So lets look at what we did.

The project team invited 30 people from marketing, production, logistics, personnel, business intelligence and of course also the R&D department for a one-day seminar. The purpose of the meeting was to identify trends that could have an impact on the focal questions. They were instructed that during the morning session they should consider the trends that would have an impact on the competences needed to develop tomorrow's products.

When this was done they were divided into groups to start evaluating the identified trends. They had two questions: how much impact would the trend have on the focal question, and how predictable was the trend? In doing this, they also put together doublets and, at the end of the process, had to agree upon the most important ones. The outcome of this short task was that at an early stage they had sorted out trends that had a low impact on the focal question as well as those had a very low predictability. They were left with the trends with high impact and high or medium-high predictability. These trends were described briefly on trend sheets and clustered with doublets from the other groups.

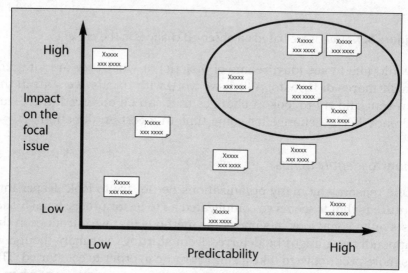

Figure 3.4. A model for a first prioritization of trends

When this was done the whole group split into sub-groups that took on the task of making a first description of the trends. They then looked deeper into the trends and tried to find examples that confirmed them. They also looked at driving forces behind the trend as well as consequences for the focal question.

In the afternoon it was time to take a closer look at the trends that would affect the ability to attract, keep and develop competence within the R&D department. The result of the day was that some 50 trends were identified. The project team took the trends and analysed them further.

Some could be eliminated as they were consequences of other trends, and others because they did not have a high enough impact. The result was some 30 trends that had a great impact on the two focal questions. Some of the trend descriptions had to be completed by the project team. Others had to be confirmed with statistics or examples.

Other methods for identifying and verifying trends

The example above illustrates an uncomplicated, straightforward way to handle questions when the organization is familiar with the area and there is a lot of knowledge about ongoing changes that can affect the focal question. Sometimes the people involved have little knowledge of the area because it is unknown. It may then be advisable to complete the intuitive inventory by using some tracking methods that go deeper. We will just mention a few of them here. A richer description can be found in the appendix.

Media scanning

Media scanning – a rapid perusal of a range of relevant articles and cuttings – is a simple and popular method for continuous cover of environmental changes and for occasional overview and inspiration at the start of a scenario planning process. A simple media scan can be a good complement to the brainstorming method we described in the example above.

Delphi

The Delphi method was invented in the 1960s and got its name from the Oracle of Delphi. The purpose from the beginning was to get quantitative future assessments through structured interviews with experts where they make judgements around different statements. The method has often been used for technical issues.

Expert panels

Many companies acquire expert panels they can consult regularly. A panel of experts will often have the role of strategic advisors whose views are considered before strategic decisions are taken.

Focus groups

Qualitative research and above all focus groups are gaining ground. In a focus group a number of people meet for one or two hours to discuss one or two specific questions. Such groups are often used when you want to get a picture of how customers or potential customers think of their future needs.

ANALYSING

The tracking phase often leaves the group with a number of separate trends covering a lot of different areas. But the trends are not as disconnected as they seem at first glance. When you look at the descriptions you often find that some trends recur as driving forces or consequences to other trends. You begin to see some patterns. Some of the identified trends may also be difficult to predict. Will they go one way or another? Will the development be slow or fast? The further the time horizon is, the more questions normally arise.

The analysing phase is about identifying drivers and consequences in order to understand how the identified trends interact. If it has not already been done, it may be fruitful to carry out a player analysis in this phase, to identify conceivable actions from other players that will affect the system. All this will give the deeper understanding that is necessary for identifying the uncertainties that the scenarios will be based upon.

In order to make the description of the analysing process more tangible we will use an example concerning combatting and preventing crime. The public prosecutor's office, the police and the crime prevention council of Sweden wanted to understand more deeply the logic of the future crime arena. It was obvious to them that major changes would be produced by changes in the environment, and that these would have an impact on the overall strategies for crime prevention in the country. One major trigger to start the scenario analysis was that, with a great number of employees getting on for retirement age, it was necessary to know what kind of competences would be particularly needed in the future.

The project was carried out by three scenario planners who took on the task along with five people from the three authorities. Four of the practitioners had a wide and deep experience, and the fifth was a person doing research into the subject. The group worked together for eight consecutive days. When we entered the process the group had identified almost 100 trends and reduced them to a total of 18. Half of the trends were comprehensive and concerned driving forces in the world outside the arena. The other half were trends that had been observed in the arena. The list of trends is shown in Figure 3.5.

The project team tried to verify all trends through statistics and other sources. Two of the trends that had been identified by representatives from the police were impossible to verify. One of them was increased consumption of alcohol; there was no evidence whatsoever of increased sale, smuggling or illicit distilling. The group decided to keep the trend anyhow as the members of the project team representing the police were very convinced. They had seen lots of examples of it the field over the last year.

Summary of trends for The Future of Crime

- There is increased internationalization.
- The European Union is getting more important.
- Values are more individualized.
- People are becoming less willing to tolerate risk.
- Society is increasingly divided.
- IT is getting better and more widespread.
- Fewer adults live as stable couples.
- Urbanization is increasing.
- Funding of public welfare is decreasing.
- The market for security products and services is increasing.
- There is increasing consumption of alcohol.
- There is greater liberalism about drugs.
- More crimes have an international aspect.
- There is increased media focus on crime and punishment.
- There are more opportunities to commit crime.
- IT related crimes have increased.
- Social constraints on active offenders have become less effective.
- During the night the city becomes a lawless zone.

Figure 3.5. Example of trends identified in a project concerning The Future of Crime

It is interesting that, a year after the scenario planning took place, statistical evidence came up which confirmed what the police officers had said. The same was true of the concept that during the night the city becomes a lawless zone; for this too a lot of evidence was uncovered over the following year.

Analysis of the interrelationships between the trends

If you want a deeper understanding of the future, it is not enough to look at the trends separately. It is when you dig deeper into the system and understand what impact trends have on each other that it becomes possible to paint pictures of the future. In order to get this deeper understanding, a cross-impact analysis was carried out. A cross-impact analysis is a method for identifying inter-relationships. Here the impact of each trend on every other trend is graded. (See 'Methods' for a more detailed description of this.)

In order to get an overview of the system a causal-loop diagram was drawn (Figure 3.6). The most dominant driving trends were put at the top and the most dependent at the bottom of the diagram. Arrows mark the direction of dependency. The shaded backgrounds show groups of trends that have much in common. (See 'Methods' for a deeper description of the causal-loop diagram).

The first and natural reaction when looking at a causal-loop diagram is confusion, but if you take some time to follow the arrows and identify the different relations, a deeper understanding will slowly emerge. In this diagram some things are obvious. The first impression might be the complexity of the relations between different trends, but a closer look will show interesting connections. Some of the most important driving forces are in the areas of internalization and IT. For example we can see that trends in these areas will accelerate the internationalization of crime. More use of alcohol, which in Sweden is very much driven by more continental drinking habits, in combination with socioeconomic trends like movements to the big cities where there is less social control and fewer people living in stable relationships, will increase the likelihood of crime. An interesting finding was that companies that provide security-oriented products and services will most probably be profitable. Knowledge of this could be of benefit for enterprises in security field. We have recently seen a rise in the stock-market valuation of such enterprises.

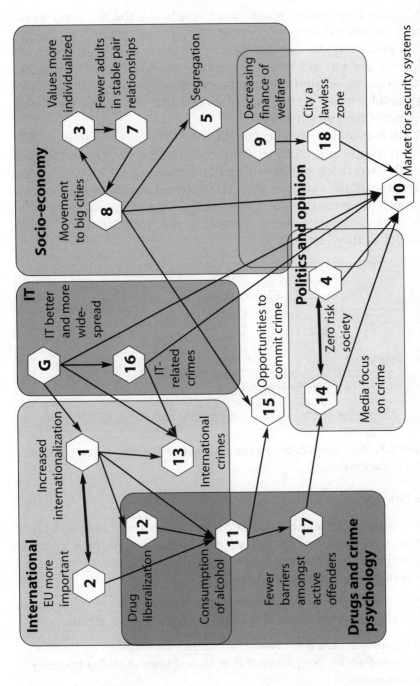

Figure 3.6. An example of a causal-loop diagram from The Future of Crime illustrating the strongest relationships between the identified trends

Building scenarios

After this preparatory stage, work starts on the scenario itself. There are several ways of proceeding, but the simplest is to begin by summarizing the 'certain' picture: in other words, what you are relatively certain will be a given future development. The qualitative reasoning around the trends and the causal-loop analysis are very helpful when setting up a timeline that illustrates the development of the certain trends.

To illustrate this, we may compare it with a play at a theatre. The certain trends and their development from the present to the year that the scenarios will depict can be compared to the back of the stage created for a certain play. The different scenarios can be seen as specific scenes that form the background of the different acts. The crime scenarios were created in the year 2000 and track changes to the year 2007.

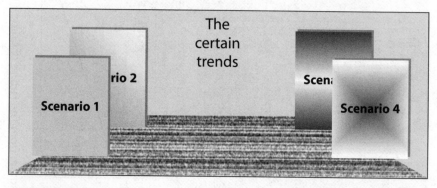

Figure 3.7. The relation between scenarios and certain trends compared with a play in the theatre

The timeline

So what may a timeline look like? It describes a probable and fairly certain development from today's date to the date of the scenarios.

If we go back to the crime scenarios the certain development for the period is outlined in Figure 3.8.

> **Figure 3.8. The timeline from the projected Future of Crime**
>
> The first seven years of the new millennium are shown to be very eventful, not least from the perspective of international integration. The following has happened:

- *In the year 2002* Sweden is a fully integrated part of the Schengen cooperation zone and the European prosecution authority Eurojust has started to function. As Sweden has become an outer border for the zone, Swedish authorities face a testing time, especially the customs, police and prosecutors. The demands of the Union have implied a tougher approach, especially towards the eastern European countries, which are not a part of the Union, at the same time as cooperation in the Baltic region has developed and deepened.
- *In 2003* a majority of the Swedish people have got broadband. This has changed society in many ways compared to the last century. In addition to the introduction of broadband, computers used in homes have become considerably faster, and the quality and quantity of communications have become substantially better and faster than before. More and more people have invested in alarm and control systems connected to the Internet.
- *In 2004* many citizens have become worried about violence on the streets. Many adults dare not go outdoors at certain times, as city centres on weekend nights are described by the daily papers as battlefields for gangs of youngsters. Anxiety about increasing consumption of alcohol in society is growing. Many people consider that the increasing consumption of alcohol, or rather the changed pattern of consumption, is caused by Sweden's adjustment to the legislation of the EU.
- *In 2005* transborder economic crime has spread as a natural consequence of European integration. Other international crimes have also grown explosively and the number of cases concerning international legal aid have multiplied since 1999.
- *In 2006* many people believe the social constraints that used to rein in active offenders have been crumbling. At the same time, while Europe and other regions of the world have become more integrated, social divisions inside nations have increased. There is hope though, as people have started to debate the causes of violence, that these causes may be better addressed. The large-scale increases in the populations of cities are seen as strong driving forces behind rootlessness and social division.
- *In 2007* it is obvious that citizens and companies have taken over more responsibility for some security functions from the state. Securitas and other companies within the field of security have multiplied their turnover in the last decade. They have gained advantage from the fact that people are increasingly unwilling to accept risks and are prepared to pay a lot for extra security. Cooperation between prosecutors and

> police from different countries has progressed positively. It is also clear that European integration and internationalization have led to some negative social consequences, for example in form of rising drug abuse. The increase in individualism and decline in collective values have probably had an influence as well.

As you can see, the timeline is built upon the certain trends and the interconnections between them. The scenario helps people to see a plausible development and the driving forces behind it without having to read 18 trends – each with a page of description – and on top of that trying to understand a causal-loop diagram. The reading of timelines also helps people to move from today into the year of the scenarios, realizing that a lot of changes have happened on the way. Understanding of these changes is essential for the understanding of the scenarios.

Scenarios and uncertainties

As we have seen in the introduction, scenarios provide a way to handle uncertainties. During the tracking phase there are often a number of trends that are likely to have a great impact on the focal question but are uncertain and not easily predictable. We do not really know if they will go one way or the other. Other trends are so uncertain that we prefer to call them wild cards. These wild cards could of course have a great impact on the focal question, but their predictability is so low that they have no meaningful use as a base for scenarios.

People very often talk of worst-case and best-case scenarios, sometimes with a scenario moderated somewhere between the two extremes. The problem is that people tend to really want only one scenario. They are likely to accept the better case and reject the worse as too bad even to consider. The result is that their view of the future may become one-dimensional and describe only one uncertainty, which may be good or bad. The dilemma is that the world of uncertainties is complex with a lot of aspects to handle.

An approach that we have found profitable, and which also is a dominating model for scenario building around the world, is to pick out two driving uncertainties that are considered together in a scenario cross. Four different scenarios will come out in the corners of the cross (Figure 3.9).

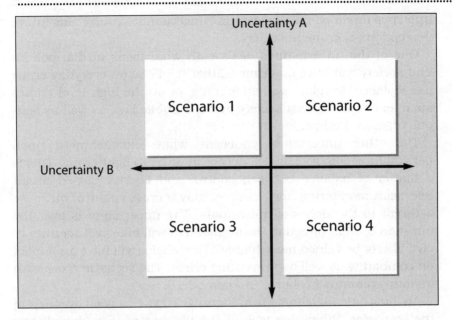

Figure 3.9. Scenario cross that constitutes four different scenarios based on two uncertainties

Of course it would be possible to construct a number of scenario crosses that illustrate many important uncertainties in different combinations. The problem with many descriptions is that people cannot keep them clearly in their minds and make any use of them. The tricky thing is to find two uncertainties that, combined with each other in a scenario cross, will give us four very different scenarios that can really help us to prepare for an uncertain future.

When you have selected a number of drivers/factors making for change, it is time to start combining them. Here you need qualitative reasoning in terms of: What will happen if this or that occurs? What developments will it lead to and what could bring it to that point? The simplest way of doing this is by systematically combining two factors at a time and adding the others on top in suitable combinations. The scenario analysis itself assumes that you use both halves of the brain, analysis as well as imagination.

When we worked with the crime scenarios, most trends felt very certain. A long track record of reported crimes showed that there had been only small changes over recent decades. The uncertainties that we decided on after testing did not deal with crime as such, but rather the perception of crime in the society. The scenarios are built upon two fundamental and genuine uncertainties concerning future perceptions of crime in society.

One of the uncertainties deals with what focus media, politics and society will have on crime. Either it will be on everyday crime like violence, burglary and shoplifting, or on the high-level crimes such as crimes against society and the public law, as well as serious organized crime.

The other uncertainty concerns what encroachment upon personal freedom society will accept in order to fight crime. This is a matter of balance between control and liberty. Closed-circuit television monitoring, for example, may increase control but pose a threat to the rights of individuals. The uncertainty is over the question of what direction the adjustment will take: will security or civil liberty be valued more highly? This choice will have an impact on combating as well as preventing crime. The scenario cross with its four scenarios is shown in Figure 3.10.

An illustration like the one in Figure 3.10 gives a good overview of the scenarios. When you look at the illustration it is immediately obvious that there are huge differences between the four scenarios. It is unlikely that any one specific scenario will turn out to be the reality in the year 2007; the Swedish crime prevention arena will probably appear as a combination of them. During the years that have passed since the scenarios were created we have seen reality move in different directions. This makes the scenarios helpful. They make it easier to foresee different environments, which is useful when it comes to strategic development and decision making.

The group that made up the scenarios could have ended their consideration when they had the scenario cross with some brief descriptions. However, the organizations that would use the scenarios in their planning processes were big, and it was essential that everyone had a chance to get a deeper understanding of what the scenarios meant. We therefore continued the work in order to make descriptions that could communicate the scenario more effectively.

Guidelines for effective scenario communication

A highly descriptive and memorable title

Memorable titles tend to be short, descriptive and distinct. It is sometimes difficult to find good titles. So it was in this case (the names we used in the crime scenarios have some kind of a deeper

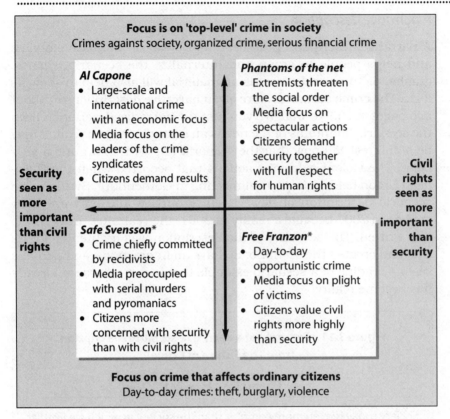

Focus is on 'top-level' crime in society
Crimes against society, organized crime, serious financial crime

Al Capone
- Large-scale and international crime with an economic focus
- Media focus on the leaders of the crime syndicates
- Citizens demand results

Phantoms of the net
- Extremists threaten the social order
- Media focus on spectacular actions
- Citizens demand security together with full respect for human rights

Security seen as more important than civil rights

Civil rights seen as more important than security

Safe Svensson*
- Crime chiefly committed by recidivists
- Media preoccupied with serial murders and pyromaniacs
- Citizens more concerned with security than with civil rights

Free Franzon*
- Day-to-day opportunistic crime
- Media focus on plight of victims
- Citizens value civil rights more highly than security

Focus on crime that affects ordinary citizens
Day-to-day crimes: theft, burglary, violence

Figure 3.10. Overview of the scenarios from The Future of Crime
* The names 'Safe Svensson' and 'Free Franzon' were chosen because they conveyed a vivid picture to the scenario participants. For different audiences, different titles should be chosen.

meaning for Swedes, although they are difficult to translate properly). Most important, though, is to avoid titles that could be perceived as judgements of good or bad.

A well-crafted storyline

A scenario is not an end-state. It is a narrative and vivid description of one possible path to the future. A compelling storyline includes answers to the fundamental questions: Who does what, with whom, when, where and why? It is important to make sure that the logic of each scenario is completely clear and differentiated from the other scenarios.

A narrative description

A narrative description puts flesh and blood on the bare storyline and helps people to grasp and internalize the scenario. Charts, graphs, pictures and other visual material will also help to show its logic. The crime scenarios were given narrative descriptions of about two pages each. We will give you just the narrative description from the scenario Phantoms of the net as an example. As you read, it may be of interest to know that the scenario was written around a year before the violent extremist actions that occurred when the European Union held an important meeting in Gothenburg, Sweden. The scenario description of how violent groups would organize their actions in 2007 became a reality in 2001, the year after the scenario was written. The accuracy of the description was frightening for us who had created the scenario. So have an interesting – and perhaps scary – reading of a scenario example that to a great extent already has become reality!

**Figure 3.11. Example of a narrative scenario description
from The Future of Crime**

Phantoms of the net

Society today is even more complex than the society in which we lived at the turn of the century, seven years ago. We have built a societal machinery that works fantastically as long as all the gearwheels revolve, but it can jam if the smallest grain of sand gets into the system.

The traditional threats to society have been handled relatively well. Organized crime has considerably less scope as a result of democratization in many countries and of active cooperation to put an end to organized crime. It has become apparent that some of these organizations were not nearly as competent as many people had supposed. Once the European countries started to tackle the problem together, it turned out to be relatively simple to limit the scope of these organizations. On the whole, the situation concerning crime against society and advanced economic crime are under control. Of course there is still a great deal of crime, but it is mostly the kind of everyday crime that we will probably live with forever.

There is however a new type of advanced crime that we have not managed to tackle at all. It comes from small but very dedicated and intelligent groups of young people who are alienated from society and see it as their task to 'unmask the violent true face of the pseudo-democratic state'.

The groups of radical vegans and squatters that we saw eight years ago seem at first glance to have some characteristics in common with similar groups of today, but there are huge differences. The young extremists of today have an entirely other kind of knowledge and lack the respect for other citizens that characterized young extremists of the past.

The young extremists are very intelligent men and women with no record of criminal convictions who in many different ways, above all through the Internet, gain knowledge that serious criminals could only dream of in the 1970s and 1980s. Knowledge is spread from group to group, from individual to individual, within a variety of areas: everything from obstructing the work of the judicature and the police, through how to produce weapons and explosives on their own, to ways of using the Internet for both collecting information and terrorist activities of various kinds. Their political habitat is very often hazy. One may talk of the left, another of anarchy and a third of Nazism. In many respects these activists seem to pick up their knowledge from the same sources, and unconventional cooperation seems more of a rule than an exception. 'The enemy of my enemy is my friend' seems to be the guiding principle, and Enemy Number One is society as a whole. The question of where they get their advanced knowledge is one that is discussed at regular intervals, but that information is spread and mediated through the Internet, is something that is commonly known.

The crimes that the media emphasize today are of two kinds: on the one hand advanced computer crimes of different kinds, on the other hand actions against real targets such as key institutions and personnel in the government and society. A single individual or just a few people with the right knowledge and tools can create huge damage; some spectacular actions have been carried out leading to great damage. We will probably never know the number of attempts that have been unsuccessful.

One of the most spectacular actions was carried out on a cold winter's night. A few people had, despite all security precautions, managed to get access to a number of the computers that regulate the Swedish electric power net. By starting a program that overloaded the internal computer network they succeeded in stopping the whole provision of electric power for a couple of hours all over Sweden. Nuclear plants had to make emergency stops and many other defects followed. It was fairly easy to identify the affected computers, but it took a long time before it was certain that no other computers had been infected.

The preventive fight against crime is very difficult as the activists often have no recorded convictions and do not stand out in a crowd from other young people in any palpable way. When crimes are committed, the perpetrators generally give themselves away in some way or other. Only a few activists have been able to carry out more than one attack before they get caught. As a result, there is no support for wiretapping and other techniques that impinge on human rights except in some very special cases. As one debater said:'in that case the police would have to wiretap all Swedes aged 19, 20 and 21; is that the kind of society we want?'

The demands of the society have instead focused on other kinds of preventive measures: partly based on supervision and protection of the most important key facilities, and partly on quick and effective reaction to the smallest sign of activity.

The demands imposed on the prosecutors and the police are, on the one hand, a fast and at the same time respectful treatment of suspects, and on the other ensuring a high level of security for their own staff, as the prosecutors themselves are an important target for many activists. The other main demands are that police and prosecutors should direct their energy towards preventing crime and that when crime happens they should be on the scene almost immediately.

At the same time concerns over human rights have a high priority and society does not want to give police and prosecutors increased opportunities for activities that can be seen as impinging on those rights.

This gives you an idea of what a narrative description can look like. There were parallel descriptions of the three other scenarios. A couple of questions to think about: Was it easy to realize what kind of environment the prosecutors and police would meet if the world turned out this way? Do you think descriptions of this kind can be helpful in risk analysis and strategic planning? The narrative descriptions do not necessarily have to be as long as this. It is though essential that they help us to see what future worlds could look like.

A table of comparable descriptions

People who like to use the creative, right half of their brain normally favour narrative descriptions. Others, who prefer to use the left half of the brain and are more analytically oriented, often prefer to have the scenarios described in a table that describes the most important differences in logics, end-states and so on. This will also give the reader of narrative descriptions a good summary of the most important differences between the scenarios. Putting the table together also gives the planner a chance to reconsider the scenarios: whether they really are qualitatively different, and if so, in what ways. On the following page you can see a couple of factors from the table for the crime scenarios.

As you can see, a table can give a good overview of the different scenarios. At this stage the group was already starting to look at the future competence needs of prosecutors and police, which was, you may recall, one of the reasons for doing the scenario analysis.

The whole scenario analysis was presented in a booklet of 100 pages. This has been used in the offices of the prosecutor, the police and the crime prevention council. Later on it was the basis for developing long-term strategies in the field.

A business-related example: daily newspapers

In the example you have just read, we chose a scenario process that dealt with the public sector. This is because our clients in the private sector do not usually like us to reveal their scenarios and strategies. In 1997, however, we were commissioned by the Swedish publishers' association to do a scenario analysis, and as this was general and did not deal with a particular newspaper we are allowed to give it as an example.

In the case of daily newspapers, the publishers' association saw that a rapid increase in demand for electronic information could cause traditional companies problems in keeping up, leading other media companies to enter the traditional domain of the daily press. The action taken by leading players would be of great importance for the further development of the industry.

A combination of two uncertain key factors for the daily newspaper industry's future gave the four scenarios sown in Figure 3.13, which were relevant for regional newspapers. In brief, they were:

- *Cyberworld 2010.* High demand and high use of technology by the newspapers. Readers quickly accept all the new technology and apparatus that the computer and telecommunications industries produce. Newspaper companies are equally quick in taking up and using the latest production and distribution technology. The technical problems that arise over the performance of computers, peripherals, accessories or digital communication, are solved as they occur.
- *Wait and see.* Consumers quickly accept technological advances as in the first scenario, while newspaper companies adopt a

Area	Al Capone	Phantoms of the net	Safe Svensson	Free Franzon
What kind of crime is focused on by the media?	Large-scale crime, crime against society.	Large-scale crime, crime against society.	Everyday crime.	Everyday crime.
Which criminals does the media focus on?	Terrorists, organized crime and advanced economic crime.	Terrorists, organized crime and advanced economic crime.	The thief, the drink driver, the rapist and the wife beater.	The thief, the drink driver, the rapist and the wife beater.
What is the driving force behind the development?	Unsuccessful fight against organized crime, etc.	Unsuccessful fight against organized crime etc. combined with abuse of power by the government.	Unsuccessful fight against everyday crime.	Unsuccessful fight against everyday crime in combination with abuse of power by the government.
What are the special demands on the prosecutors?	Competence within international jurisdiction, languages, IT and supervision techniques.	Competence in dealing with young people and values. Quick handling of cases, respect for all suspects. High level of security for the prosecutors themselves.	Competence in psychology, psychiatry, technical supervision and perpetrator profiling.	Being near the scene of a crime, quick and effective response, and respect for all suspects.
What are the special demands on the police?	Collect and handle key information from, for example, wiretapping.	Preventive action and quick at the scene of a crime.	Collect and handle key information from, for example, wiretapping.	Preventive action and quick at the scene of a crime.

Figure 3.12. Extract from the scenario comparison concerning The Future of Crime

sceptical attitude towards the newfangled ideas. There is a demand for digital content that the newspapers do not meet. New global players enter the scene.

- *Business as usual.* This is a scenario marked by great conservatism about the form of the papers and how they are produced. Both the newspapers and their readers are highly sceptical of the newfangled technology. They know what they've got, but not what they'll get.
- *High-tech production.* Consumers are not inclined to accept innovation in the form of new technology, whether it is for entertainment, education, news or amusement. The printed newspaper is the main medium for news and all other values the paper has today. On the other hand, newspapers take advantage of every opportunity technology can offer in making production of printed papers more efficient.

The scenarios and the timeline behind them were warmly welcomed by the publishers, who realized that changes were coming. The editors and journalists on the other hand were very conservative and thought that electronic media could never break the power of the newspapers. The scenarios caused the biggest debate ever in *The*

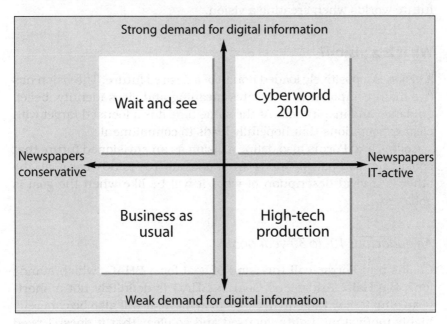

Figure 3.13. Four scenarios on the future of daily newspapers

Paper, the trade journal of the press. Publishers stood on one side and editors and journalists on the other. The various arguments included the unforgettable line: 'Who could wrap up a fish in an electronic paper?' It took three years before we had an assignment from one of the newspapers. By then some of the developments, among others declining advertising revenue, that had been described in the timeline had become real. Then it was high time to take action!

IMAGING

The parts of TAIDA described so far deal with probable futures. We have tracked changes in the environment, analysed them and created alternative future scenarios. It has had nothing to do with what we want to see and achieve. Now it is time to take a look at what we can do to create pictures of a desired future. This is where we engage ourselves in what we really want and create visions. Of course it is quite possible to create a vision for the future without going through the previous steps. But what we have done so far helps us to understand what the future world may look like. That awareness can help us to free ourselves from the present environment and move into future worlds when creating a vision.

What is a vision?

A vision is a positively loaded notion of a desired future. The vision has two main components. It creates meaning and gives identity, belief, guidance and inspiration. At the same time it is a focused target with clear expectations that hopefully leads to commitment.

Collins and Porras also define a vision as an envisioned future that consists of two parts. One is an audacious 10- to 30-year goal, the other is a vivid description of what it will be like when the goal is achieved.

An audacious 10- to 30-year goal

Collins and Porras call this kind of goal for a BHAG, which stands for a Big Hairy Audacious Goal. A BHAG is definitely not a short-term aim; it may take up decades to achieve. It will also be concrete, highly motivating, tightly focused and so clear that it doesn't need any further description.

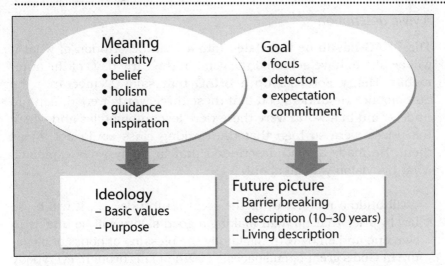

Figure 3.14. The components of a vision
Source: Based on a figure by Collins and Porras (1996).

A vision requires a special type of BHAG: a vision-level BHAG that applies to the entire organization and requires 10–30 years of effort to complete. It is tangible, energizing, and highly focused. It does not have to be further described. People get it right away. It also engages people: it reaches out and grabs them. A BHAG should not be a sure bet – it will have perhaps only a 50 per cent to 70 per cent probability of success – but the organization must believe that it can reach the goal.

BHAGs can be quantitative as well as qualitative. An example of a qualitative BHAG is when Sony in the early 1950s stated its intention to 'become the company best known for changing the worldwide poor-quality image of Japanese products'. A quantitative example is when Wal-Mart in 1990 said that they would become a 125 billion dollar company by the year 2000. Other BHAGs can focus on a common enemy, often a bigger player on the market. This was the case when Nike in the 1960s said that they would crush Adidas. In some cases, they may be expressed in terms of role models, as when Stanford University in the 1940s said that they would become the Harvard of the west.

Internal transfer BHAGs are often used in large, established organizations. This is what Rockwell did in 1995 when they said they would 'transform this company from a defence contractor into the best-diversified high-technology company in the world'.

A vivid description

The BHAG has to be translated into a vivid description of what it will be like to have achieved the goal. In the early days of the automobile, Henry Ford set up a BHAG that said: 'Democratize the automobile!' He understood that these three words were difficult to understand in a world were there were few automobiles and where the prices were so high that the working class could not afford them. He made a vivid description that in many ways explained what his vision was all about:

> I will build a motor car for the great multitude. . . . It will be so low in price that no man making a good salary will be unable to own one and enjoy with his family the blessing of hours of pleasure in God's great open spaces. . . . When I'm through, everybody will be able to afford one, and everyone will have one. The horse will have disappeared from our highways, the automobile will be taken for granted . . . [and we will] give a large number of men employment at good wages.

It is obvious that the vivid description makes it easier to understand the meaning of the three words. And as we all know he succeeded in reaching his goal!

How to create a vision

As we have already mentioned a vision is a deeply desired picture of the future. It is like a dream that we want with all our hearts to become true in a distant future. Visions deal very much with feelings and emotions. They bring us into contact with our deepest wishes. This makes it impossible to attack them with analytical methods. Intuition and creativity are the most essential assets when we try to understand our real desires. But if you feel more that you are an analyst, your hour will come when it is time to find and clarify the essence of the vision.

Let us follow a case where we worked together with a division of a multinational industry and see what we did. The methods we used are among the most effective, while they are also simple to use. It might be worth mentioning that there had been a Tracking and Analysing process, with around 30 participants from different countries, before the vision process started.

The vision seminar

A group of 50 people, representing all kinds of functions from different parts of the organization, were invited to a workshop. They met from lunchtime one day to lunch the following day. After an introduction that included a presentation of the scenarios and a short lecture on the need for visions, the process started. The first task was individual. After an orientation session where they were guided to leave the present and gradually transport themselves into an imaginary world ten years in the future, they were asked to write a personal letter to a former colleague. It should be written and dated ten years into the future and they had one hour for the writing.

Most people really enjoy writing letters like this. The format is perfect as all people have an experience of writing a letter to a friend. And in a letter you automatically tell stories that are vivid.

After the letters were written the participants met in groups to find the common denominators that they observed. When the presentations took place everyone was amazed over the similarities among what came up in the group presentations. The lists as well as the letters were collected by the project team.

The creation of the vision

Directly after the seminar the project team started to deal with the material. The presentations at the seminar showed that there were a number of cornerstones. The group read all the letters and found a couple more things that had been mentioned frequently, but which hadn't been mentioned in the presentations. Altogether there were 15 cornerstones. The team used a single-impact analysis to check how well the cornerstones corresponded with the analysis made of the future environment, and they also performed a number of other analyses.

It was, however, difficult for the group to decide which were the most important cornerstones. A cross-impact analysis was carried out and a causal-loop diagram was drawn. The diagram showed very clearly that there were four cornerstones that acted as spiders in the net. If the focus was put on those four, it would give energy to the others.

Finally the group ended up with a BHAG and four cornerstones. This was accompanied by a vivid description. As the participants had written letters from the future and told their colleagues in their workplaces about the experience, the project team decided to use the letter format for the vivid description. There were also many creative and exiting formulations in the letters from the seminars that could be used in the final letter. And, automatically, they had a lot of ambassadors who really felt they were a part of creating the vision.

Some experiences of visions

Reality checks

Many visions tend to be pie in the sky. This can be avoided with a reality check. Does the history of the organization support the vision? Does the vision help the organization to meet plausible future changes in the environment? A vision that is reality checked will more easily be accepted and easier to realize.

Challenging vision

A vision has to be challenging. If not, people will read it and dismiss it with a yawn. There is a problem though. If the challenge is so big that people do not think it will ever be possible to meet it, the vision is unworkable. It borders on insanity. On the other hand if the organizations think they are almost there, it is under-stimulating. The risk of a yawn or at least no real effort is big if the vision is within the comfort zone. The ideal vision is normally a barrier breaker, challenging but not totally impossible to reach (Figure 3.15).

Over-communicate the vision

Those who have been engaged in the development of the vision often know it by heart. What they may fail to consider is that a mere presentation at a company meeting is not enough to make the vision a real directing guideline for the future that is shared by everyone. To achieve a shared vision it is necessary to disseminate it in every department and show what it means for that specific workplace and its people, as well as to work intensely to remove obstacles that obstruct movement in the right direction.

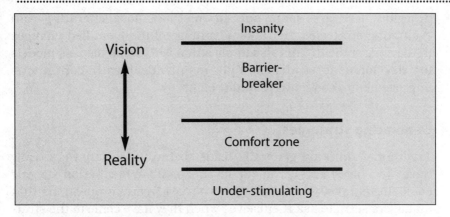

Figure 3.15. The tension between vision and reality

Strategies, goals and supporting actions

The strategies of the company must support the vision. If not, no one will believe that the vision has any true meaning. Short-term goals and actions in the direction of the vision are also important if the vision is to inspire trust.

DECIDING

Deciding is the phase where everything is put together. The future environment is tracked and analysed and the vision is in place. What can be done to go in the direction of the vision, taking advantage of the opportunities and avoiding the threats of the future environment?

We will consider here methods that we have found successful when dealing with a complex environment that is changing rapidly. We have gradually developed the methods as we have worked with companies whose business environment has been radically transformed. They have realized that the industry standards within their field, which has been prosperous for a long time, will soon be outdated. Sometimes the changes have been so big that it has been possible to predict a coming paradigm shift. The problem has then often been that it has been easy to see a paradigm shift would come, but difficult to know what the new paradigm would look like or what strategies would prosper in it. It has become very obvious to these companies that traditional methods are inadequate. So what we will describe here are some specific methods for generating and evaluating strategies that take advantage of the identified changes in the environment. This also implies that we will not discuss models for development strategies that mainly deal with continuous improvements, cost cutting and the like.

Generating strategies

Traditional thinking generally leads to traditional answers. How have we solved this problem in the past? What action do our competitors take? Those are the two most frequent questions that managers seem to ask themselves when they have come to the strategy part of the business plan. One manager expressed it this way: 'When you finally, after long discussions, have decided on mission, vision and long-term goals, there is little time left for strategic work. Then it is very likely that you'll pull open the third drawer where you keep your old strategies and some examples from different parts of the industry.' Others say that they discuss the situation on an overall level and try to find a good strategy that works.

The problem is that you often have to find new answers to new questions. And when a new strategy is beginning to evolve, there is no framework to put the answers in, and no agreed way to label them. This is an effective barrier to new thinking. If we want to find new strategies we have to abandon top-down thinking and start to think bottom-up. This means that we have to start with small ideas for solutions, and from that starting point build up the jigsaw puzzle until new patterns show. These patterns can become the embryos of new strategies. But the ideas have to come from somewhere. What we prefer to use as inspiration is what has come up in the trend and scenario analyses.

Trends as input for generating strategies

The certain trends that were identified during the tracking phase are a very good starting point when we want to create new strategies. They are the keystones of the 'certain future' and have been described in such detail that they will serve as a solid jumping-off point for our imagination.

Their use may be clarified by a recent example from the food industry. In this case the industry wanted to identify new business possibilities that could meet changing demands and eating habits.

They had done a thorough study of trends in the tracking phase and identified 12 clusters of trends that they considered would have a great impact on the industry. They assembled a group of product developers and marketing specialists who met for a one-day workshop. The task was to find new product ideas that would be competitive in tomorrow's world.

The group broke up into smaller groups of three or four people. They considered four trends each. The task was to take one trend at a time in order to understand its logic and deeper consequences. To be able to take in the whole situation, they used a consequence-tree to substantiate their findings (Figure 3.16).

The consequence tree represents a coherent system of driving forces, clusters of trends and consequences. The driving forces are the root system and help show why a trend may develop in a particular way. The trend or trend-cluster constitutes the trunk. Height and thickness give us a hint of the development of the trend so far. The consequences of the trend are shown as branches. Think of the first, second and third-level consequences. The crown of the tree shows the complexity of the development and its connections. When the group members had compiled the tree they started to generate product ideas that they wrote down on sticky notes. The notes were clustered and the clusters described. The result of the process was a number of new products and product segments that originated

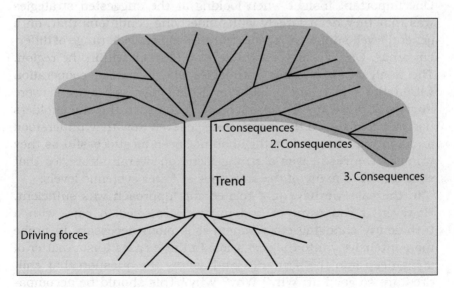

Figure 3.16. A consequence tree

from the trends. Such stimulants for ideas are very useful when you are setting out upon unknown paths.

Scenarios as input for generating strategies

A common way to use scenarios as inputs for strategic work is to analyse what the success factors will be in the various scenarios. Together with an analysis of the assets of the company, it is easy to draw simple pictures that show both the common denominators of the scenarios and what it is that separates one from another.

When we did this in a project concerning a region of Sweden, it became very obvious that there were very different success factors in the different scenarios. One scenario, which showed a development very much on familiar and well-developed lines, did not require new strategies; it would be enough to improve some of the old paths. The other three scenarios showed that the stakeholders had to start working on some completely new strategies if they were to succeed. The analysis of one scenario in particular showed enormous challenges. Some of the strategies were very similar in the different scenarios and others were very specific to one particular scenario. For each scenario, a simple GAP analysis showed the gap between demands and assets. This analysis, together with some others, became the basis for creating strategy suggestions. One important insight when looking at the suggested strategies was that they dealt largely with underlying conditions that, on a general level, supported specific strategies in a wide range of different areas. One strategy was to develop tourism within the region. The analysis showed that strategies like increased cooperation within the region and greater pride amongst the citizens were important prerequisites for success. Up till then the stakeholders had only focused on the lower strategic level. Now they understood an important reason why they had not been as successful as they wanted. The result was a strong focus on overall strategies that contributed to many of the strategies at lower systemic levels.

In the case we have just related this approach was sufficient. However, if you want to find unique strategies to cope with a turbulently changing environment it is often necessary to probe more intensively into the scenarios. In these cases it is a matter of going deep into the scenarios and asking the question that children are so good at: Why? Why? Why? This should be accompanied by looking at the consequences, and the consequences of the consequences, in a similar manner to that described in the trend example above. Even here it is very important to write down all ideas that come up in order to be able to cluster them later on.

Core competences or other assets as input for generating strategies

Another starting point can be the core competences of the organization. Once one has a clear awareness of trends and scenarios, it can be good to look at one core competence or asset at a time and look at the scenarios and trends (which may be shown, for example on wall charts), and see what ideas will come up. Note all the ideas, without making any judgements, for clustering later on. This will help you to look at the strengths of your organization from a new angle.

Visions as input for generating strategies

Of course the vision can be a source of inspiration for new ideas. The process can be similar to the one we described for core competences.

Clustering ideas into embryonic strategies

At this point it is easy to feel lost amongst hundreds of suggestions, on a very often detailed level. The purpose of the bottom-up strategy is, as we have mentioned before, to use the ideas as building blocks that can help us see patterns that no one else has observed before. At this stage it is time to gather together all the ideas that have come up, whether they came from trends, scenarios, core competences or visions. Cluster all the ideas on a big wall chart and frame the patterns that appear (Figure 3.17). Try to see new patterns that have not been obvious before. It is important to label them explicitly. Traditional labels like 'marketing' or 'human resource development' are too woolly to show any specific direction.

Looking at the clusters may reveal new patterns. You will often not be sure that particular suggestions are the best ones, but many suggestions pointing in one direction can give a hint that there is scope for more ideas of the same kind. It is probably worthwhile to describe and make a first evaluation of the cluster. Give these clusters names that speak for themselves and a description of a couple of lines. This is absolutely essential for the next step: the evaluation.

Figure 3.17. The clustering process

Evaluation of strategy suggestions

To evaluate strategies thoroughly can be very time consuming and expensive. At this stage it is important to get a good overview of strategies that may qualify for deeper analysis. Profitable strategies tend to be effective in meeting the challenges of the environment, utilize the strengths of the organization and, finally, help us to go in the desired direction.

WUS analysis

A WUS analysis is a single-impact analysis that deals with the three dimensions (Want, Utilize and Should). It will give a fairly quick answer to three questions:

- Does the strategy contribute to the desired direction of the organization (Want)?
- Does it utilize present strengths or assets of the organization (Utilize)?
- Does it match the future environment (Should)?

In the WUS analysis the suggested strategies, sometimes accompanied with some already existing, are quantitatively evaluated on the basis of criteria from the three areas (Figure 3.18). The strategy suggestions are put on one axis in a matrix and the evaluation criteria on the other. The project team will evaluate each strategy separately against each of the criteria. Yes, it takes some time! But it is quicker than you first think, as all the evaluations are intuitive on a four-point scale.

A couple of years ago we did a WUS evaluation for a company in the service sector and we ran into some interesting findings. Various new and some old strategies were analysed and the result was the one shown in Figure 3.19.

Understandably, the client has not allowed us to reveal the actual strategies, but it is still easy to draw some conclusions just from looking at the graph. The strategies that were most essential in order to meet the challenges from the environment did not make much use of the present assets. The same went for many of the strategies that supported the vision. It is interesting that Strategy Number Five, which utilized the assets best, neither supported the vision nor met the challenges posed by the environment. This strategy had been one of the dominant approaches in the company for a couple of decades. The discovery was very useful, though extremely unpleasant. It was some consolation, however, that many of the techniques that this strategy was based upon could be transformed in such a way that they would still be useful in the future.

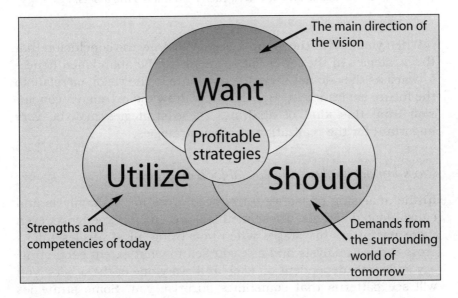

Figure 3.18. The WUS model

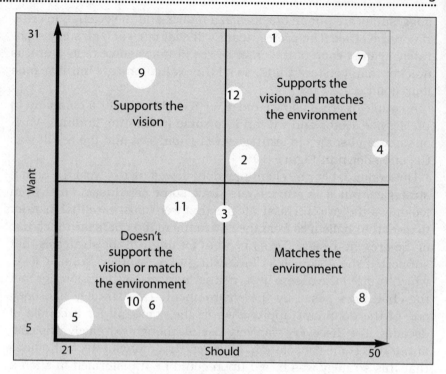

Figure 3.19. Example of WUS analysis in a service-sector company
The size of the circles shows how well each item utilizes the assets.

When you look at the graph it is easy to draw the conclusion that the strategies in the lower left segment can be abandoned henceforward as they do not seem to contribute to the vision or relate to the future environment. But that is to draw too extreme a conclusion from this kind of analysis. These strategies may be very important for the realization of other strategies.

Cross-impact analysis and causal-loop diagrams

In the analysing phase we introduced cross-impact analysis and causal-loop diagrams. Those methods are, in our experience, even more useful at this stage. When you bring all strategies into a cross-impact analysis and ask yourself to what extent each strategy is directly dependent on each and every one of the others, you will see patterns that sometimes surprise you. Some strategies that seem to have no importance at all when we look at the result from the WUS analysis turn out to be absolute prerequisites for most other strategies.

This was very apparent in a company within the finance sector. Twenty strategies had been identified and a WUS analysis had already been done. A cross-impact analysis was the next step. When a causal-loop diagram was drawn with the most driving strategies on top and the most dependent at the bottom (see Figure 3.20) it was apparent that almost all other strategies were directly or indirectly extremely dependent on a specific leadership strategy (marked as '20' in the figure). It is interesting to note that this strategy had not come up in the strategy generation phase. It was incorporated into the analysis as a result of previous experience with other companies that had shown us that such a strategy is normally important for success. The client was not particularly interested in bringing it into the analysis, as the overall concern

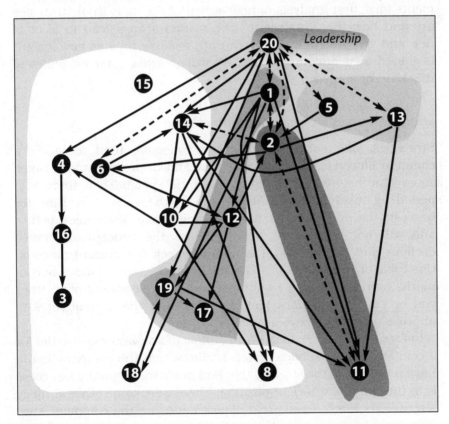

Figure 3.20. Example of causal-loop diagram used for strategy analyses

was not with leadership. The WUS analysis showed low scores in all three aspects. The result of the cross-impact analysis shown in Figure 3.20 was very important to the successful completion of the project. It also explained why earlier attempts had failed!

The shaded fields mark strategic areas with many related strategies. They helped us to summarize the strategies into five comprehensive strategic areas that were easy to communicate.

The causal-loop diagram can also be helpful when it is time to plan the implementation of the different strategies. Strategy 15 can be handled without much concern for the others. Most of the strategies, however, are very dependent on each other.

Complementary analyses

The analyses that we have just described are the primary requirements for a first analysis of how essential the individual strategies are and how they interrelate. The results always lead to a lot of new and very useful insights. But at the same time as new insight is gained, new questions arise. We will give you some examples of this kind of analyses.

Strategies versus life cycle and competitors

Strategies, and especially business concepts, tend to follow a common life cycle. They start as new and unproven, and it takes some time before the development gains speed. Then there is a period of steady growth. At the top of the cycle it is time for harvest; the prospects for high earnings have never been better, and will not improve in the future as the concept stagnates, declines and finally dies. It is wise to check the present place on this cycle of your strategies and business concepts. This is particularly interesting if you combine it with an assessment of whether you or your competitors have (or can have) the prerequisites to improve or even achieve a unique position.

In Figure 3.21 you can see an example of an evaluation we did for a company in the service sector. It shows that the company had a huge problem, as the strategy that had made the company a success is in the extreme top-right position. There were some other strategy suggestions that offered great opportunities for the company; they were more likely to succeed than those of the competitors, and they were also at the stage where the development was gaining speed and

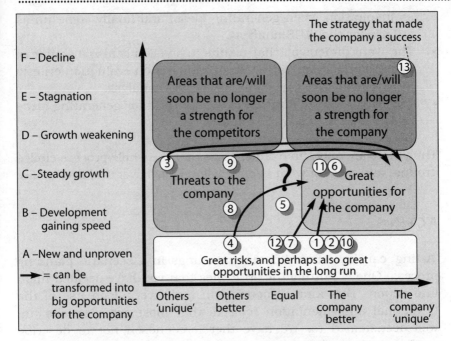

Figure 3.21. Strategies versus life cycle: an example from the service industry

could be accelerated. The competitors had certain advantages when it came to other strategies at the same stage of the development cycle; these strategies could be adopted by the company, but there would be a great deal of work to be done to catch up with the competition. Then there were some high-risk strategies that might offer advantages in due course, but they were new and as yet unproven. This analysis of course needs to be deepened, but it provides a good foundation for further discussions.

An overview of the system

Having come this far, you might think that it is a very complicated journey with lots of different components. It is easier than it seems at first sight. If you look at Figure 3.22 it will be obvious how work done at the beginning of the process will be used over and over again, and that the work is consequently built upon the three dimensions: Want, Utilize and Should.

- If we start with the Should dimension, the trends are used as a basis for scenarios. Both trends and scenarios are then used as inspiration when generating ideas, and finally come up as criteria for the WUS analysis.

- The Want dimension that results in a vision is also a source of inspiration for generating ideas and later on evaluation criteria for the strategy suggestions in the WUS analysis.
- Finally the Utilize dimension can be used for generating ideas and criteria in the WUS analysis.

Thus there are only three dimensions that the whole process circles around, and most of what is done will be used over and over again.

ACTING

'Acting' can have two different meanings in a scenario planning process. One is putting the strategies that you have decided upon into action. This kind of action can make very good use of the traditional implementation toolsets that most organizations are well accustomed to. We have therefore chosen not to describe implementation of chosen strategies here.

The other meaning has to do with the continuous follow-up work of the scenario planning process: monitoring environmental changes, defining processes for continuous environmental scanning, scenario planning and so on. Many of these acting aspects are beyond the scope of this book, but the key issues will be highlighted.

As you will understand, a lot of work is usually necessary in order to identify trends and create scenarios. If you have followed the process through and used the scenarios in vision processes or strategic work, you probably feel that you have made good use of all the united efforts in the scenario process, and perhaps think that you will not need to do this again for some years. What you forget is that you have an immense amount of basic structured and pedagogical information that can easily be put to use in current planning. Let us first have a look at how trends and scenarios can be used.

Early warning

Scenarios can be very helpful when we want to check where the environment is heading. Early warning systems help us to observe and analyse drivers in the environment that indicate if we are headed towards one scenario or another. These systems

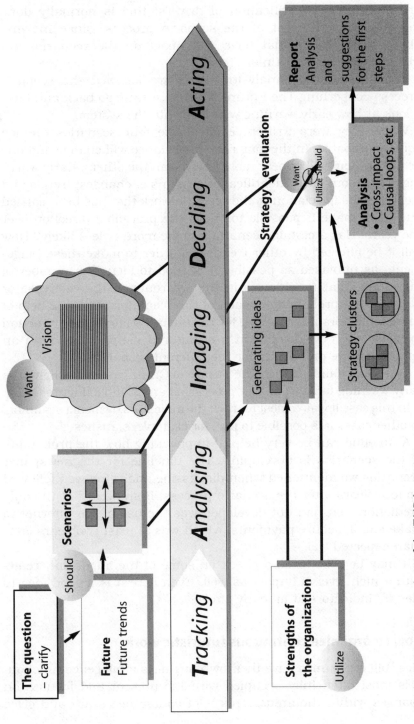

Figure 3.22. An overview of the TAIDA process

are built upon identification of drivers; this is normally done together with the rest of the scenario process, since insights about mechanisms that have an impact on the scenarios are highly salient at that time.

In discussing the analysing phase we followed the scenario process concerning The Future of Crime. Let us go back and have a look at how early warning was built into the system.

When they were written, each of the four scenarios seemed equally probable. In the long run this balance will change and one or two of them will appear more likely than the others. Early warning is all about early identification of signs of changes, trends and trend breaks in relation to the scenario work that has been carried out. They make it possible to check the prevailing direction over the years. Has a certain scenario become more or less likely? How will it be affected by other trends? In order to make these judgements as unbiased as possible it is good to identify a number of indicators; that is, changes in the environment that increase or decrease the probability of each of the scenarios. With the help of these indicators it is possible for the business intelligence function to follow the development in a structured manner and form an opinion on the probability for the different scenarios.

As you are familiar with The Future of Crime case we will give the early warning table from that process as an example (Figure 3.23).

In this case it was easiest to track the indicators by media scanning. In other cases it is possible to use, for example, statistics.

A timeline can be very helpful in checking how the probability of the scenarios is developing. The timeline for the newspaper scenarios we mentioned when discussing analysing was followed up four years after the scenario process. It showed that the only prediction that had not developed was the use of the Internet to make small, secure payments, which was at least two years later than expected.

It may be wise to do a check on some of the important trends with a high level of impact as well. Even here it is a good idea to identify indicators at an early stage.

How to organize continuous futuristic work

Most big companies have their own business intelligence function. It is most often fully occupied with the present and focuses on changes within the arena. This is of course necessary and gives

	Al Capone	Phantoms of the net	Safe Svensson	Free Franzon
Success in tackling international terror groups			++	++
Success in tackling economic crime			++	++
Increased demands for protection of civil rights		++		++
Increased demands for closed-circuit TV systems in society	++		+++	
Increased demands for effective action against large-scale organized crime	+++	++		
Increased demands for protection of ordinary citizens			++	++
Increased focus on the situation of the victims of crime		+	++	++
Scandals concerning client databases		+		+
Young activists with far reaching knowledge carrying out extensive actions	+	+++		
Unmasking of corruption amongst people at the top of society	+	++		+
New cases of 'serial killers' showing up			+++	
Antagonism between Swedes and immigrants where it is claimed that immigrants are inclined to commit crime			++	

Figure 3.23. Overview of a number of examples of occurrences in the environment that have an impact on the probability of the realization of the different scenarios

Note: The number of plus symbols indicates to what extent the indicator applies to each scenario.

good information on changes within the company's own field. The problem is that it is too short-sighted and it is often too late to start acting when competitors have already seized the initiative.

There is no one simple answer on how to organize continuous futuristic work. It depends very much on culture, resources and similar factors. We will therefore give an example that describes the situation of one of our clients and how they handled it.

A dominating actor within the food sector had for some time had a number of people tracking developments in fields such as politics, technology, social changes and so forth. This was producing a lot of information, but it was neither collated nor properly spread to parts of the organization that could make use of it. What they did was to organize the people working with the information and add some people covering blind spots. The starting point for the new group was a workshop where they did an overall analysis of the environment. They decided upon areas to be covered and defined the central business intelligence function as the 'spider' in a web of people who watched different areas. Findings were rapidly mailed to the people who needed the information. Once a quarter they met to analyse all their findings and to produce a more comprehensive quarterly report.

In order to raise interest in future issues they organized a series of seminars for people from various parts of the organization. At these seminars the participants undertook their own intuitive scanning of trends and analysed the consequences for the organization. This increased people's interest in being updated on the results that the group produced. The group also received many tips on phenomena and changes that were worth considering more deeply.

TWENTY-FOUR PITFALLS

We had a professor at college who would repeatedly ask the question: What can you learn from this experience? And it has become a habit for us to ask that question, as it is open and reveals both good and bad experiences.

Over the years we have ourselves led or been involved in a great number of scenario planning projects. We have also followed a lot of projects involving our colleagues at Kairos Future. In addition, clients have shared their experiences with us. Some of the good experiences have been mirrored through the examples in

Chapter 3. Here we will give you the two dozen most important pitfalls as we see them.

Preparation

Unclear purpose

A process may start with an unclear purpose. It might, for example, begin as a narrowly based process involving chiefly experts focusing on strategy; then all of a sudden it becomes apparent that the essential need is for a broad involvement of the organization's personnel in order to increase awareness of the need for renewal. It should have been a scenario learning rather than a scenario planning project.

Woolly questions

The focal question for the scenario planning may be too woolly. This often leads to an all-embracing tracking of trends that often leaves more specific and important trends aside. Later on, when it becomes obvious that some important trends have been ignored, much of the analysing work based on the trends has to be redone, and this holds up the process.

Inappropriate timeframe

Most often the proposed timeframe is too short. The trends and scenarios are to be used for planning purposes for only the next few years. A timeframe shorter than five years hinders observation of central trends; important changes cannot be predicted on such a short scale. At the other end of the spectrum, too long a timeframe often leads to unfounded speculation.

A team with a narrow perspective

A team whose participants all come from inside the organization often tends to take an inside–out perspective. Too much attention will be given to their own organization and the field they are working in. Long-term changes in the field often develop as consequences of driving forces in the environment outside it, and these will not be identified. The composition of a participatory scenario group should be heterogeneous as well as balanced.

Tracking

Identifying trends not based on observed change

Trends that are not based on observed changes tend to be either nightmares or daydreams. They most often occur as a result of a process-based work when very little focus has been laid on completion and description of the trends.

Too narrow a perspective

Looking at trends on a high enough systemic level is not sufficient guarantee for a broad perspective. It is often good to use a check-list that makes it easier to observe changes in systems that are otherwise easily overlooked.

Too many trends

Too many trends often come up. Some people have difficulty in turning their attention away from trends that have been identified but that are not particularly important because they have low predictability and a low level of impact on the focal question. Some trends can be driving forces or consequences to other trends, and can therefore be consolidated under a single heading.

Not supporting the trends with evidence

In many industries there are some eternal truths that are constantly cultivated. People tend to say that 'this is the way it is'. Many times it is not that way. No one has bothered to check the real truth. It is surprising how often there is no evidence of trends that people claim they are sure of. So look for evidence!

Analysing

Inability to identify the most relevant uncertainties

Uncertainties on too low a systemic level do not have a big enough impact on the system to create scenarios that are different from each other in more than one or two aspects. An uncertain trend that has a great impact on many other trends will lead to more different consequences for the system being studied. It is of similar importance to find the uncertainties that are most important for the focal question.

Scenarios based on uncertainties that are not really uncertain

It can be tempting to use a scenario axis that is not really uncertain but gives very interesting scenarios in combination with another axis. This easily happens when there is not enough time for scenario building or when the issue is very difficult. Sometimes a productive scenario cross is found immediately, but most often it takes at least a day or two to find the right combination of uncertainties.

Scenarios that are detailed, but not comprehensive

Creative writers can easily produce a long description that fascinates the reader. These may only mirror a very narrow perspective however. A comparison table based on trends or identified important factors used as a check list for the narrative description will enhance the comprehensiveness of the scenarios.

Scenarios that are too general

The scenarios may be described on too general a level that is not relevant for the question. It is easy to become fascinated with descriptions of the world at a high systemic level. What is relevant for the organization is most often found in comprehensible patterns discerned in its field, and analysis of their consequences for the actual development of the organization. Tailoring these patterns to fit the purpose makes them useful.

Imaging

Pie in the sky

The vision may seem so remote that it is conceived of as a free-floating fantasy that the organization can never realize. Sometimes the vision bears little relation to the probable future environment. This is one of the reasons why a scenario process constitutes a good start for a vision project.

Lack of participation in the vision process

Visions built solely by a few members of the top management tend to stay on the bookshelves. If people from the organization have been a part of the vision process, it can be made concrete much more easily. The vision will also far better reflect people's thoughts.

Not communicating the vision enough

Many people seem to think that a vision will inspire and guide once it is printed in a fancy folder. Under-communication is the most frequent reason why visionary leadership fails. Communicate over and over again and relate strategies and actions to the vision whenever they are discussed.

Not living the vision

Strategies, goals and actions often seem to be set without any relation to the vision, and nothing is done to remove obstacles to a new vision. Obviously the top management has to be very consistent in living the vision. Then it will rub off on the rest of the organization.

Deciding

Standard answers to non-standard environments

People often fail to realize that it takes both time and a systematic process to find strategies that are not already in common use. Few people realize that the result of a scenario planning process can provide lot of ideas for new strategies and solutions.

It feels safe to cling on to old strategies

It is very easy to cling on to old strategies that have served well in the past. It seems that organizations will not accept they must find new paths until it has been proven time after time that their old strategies do not work in the face of change.

Not translating long-term strategies into short-term developments

A strategy will not produce results until real changes have been made in areas such as work processes. It takes a lot of energy to change a well-established work pattern into a new one. This emphasizes the need to involve middle-management in strategy development and follow-up.

Implementing work patterns that meet future changes too soon

A particular strategy or solution may be very good at meeting a future change. But the future is not here yet. Market analyses do not give good answers about how tomorrow's consumer will react, but they can give a very good answer about how today's consumers will respond to a new product.

Acting

Business intelligence only focuses on competitors' actions

The business intelligence function may be too narrowly focused and only consider changes made by competitors and customers. A wider scanning and a deeper analysis can give earlier warnings on changes that can affect the company.

Low endurance

The people involved in scanning the environment often do it as a part-time job. The risk is obvious that they will give priority to other tasks that are more highly valued in the organization. It is obvious that scanning must be accorded a greater value.

The information is only used by a few

There are many organizations that have databases filled with information. The problem is that very few people know that it exists, and even fewer have the knowledge needed to use it.

The future is forgotten

During a scenario process, a strong focus is put on the future and the challenges that it provides. When the process is over people go back to the everyday questions that tend to be placed on top of the in-tray. The danger is that the future issues will not get to the top of the pile until too late.

The Principles of Scenario Thinking

In the previous chapters we have introduced the arguments for scenario planning, given a brief background and introduction, and provided an in-depth description of scenario planning in practice. In Chapters 4 and 5 we will summarize the content of book in a few principles of scenario and strategy thinking.

THE SEVEN PRINCIPLES OF SCENARIO THINKING

As the observant reader will already have noticed, scenario thinking is based upon a number of principles. These can easily be summarized in *seven* fundamental perspectives applied to specific questions or decision tasks.

- The very first principle we simply call '*Get yourself a toolbox*'. It is easy to believe that thinking is just about thinking. But the general experience is that thinking can and has to be improved by techniques, methods, tools. So, use tools and get yourself a well-equipped toolbox!
- The second principle is called '*Handle your brain with care*'. The brain is a fantastic tool, which should be treated with respect. It has developed over eons and thus adopted several principles for survival and success. Those should be known, respected and used.
- Third, scenario thinking is based on a view of the world as a drama where each player is dependent on and influences all other players on the scene. To *think in dramas* is the overall perspective that contains all other fundamental perspectives such as thinking in futures, systems thinking, uncertainty thinking, actor thinking and thinking about your moves.
- *Thinking in futures* is the pure essence of scenario thinking. Thinking in futures means putting the future first. Starting

with what might happen, and from that imagined future, plan for what to do.

- Fifth, scenario thinking is about *thinking in uncertainties*. Managing uncertainty is, as Thompson pointed out, the main task for any managerial process.
- *Thinking in systems* means thinking from the outside in, thinking in levels and inter-connections, independence and dependencies.
- Finally, the link from scenario to strategy runs through *strategic* moves. Moves are taken by others, but also by your own organization. From the drama perspective, strategy is about intentions, interventions, actions and strategic moves.

PRINCIPLE 1: GET YOURSELF A TOOLBOX

Philosophers throughout history have known that you need tools, principles and methods to improve your thinking. The whole tradition of academic training is also about teaching students to use appropriate tools.

Scenario planning is by nature a multi-disciplinary field, dealing with extremely complex issues. The mission is to develop maps of the present and the future that are relevant to management. To do that there is a need for methods and tools to:

- identify emerging trends and potential issues
- identify their consequences and conceivable reactions to them
- generate alternative scenarios and images of the future.

Quantitative and qualitative methods are necessary at different times. Some questions may be solved by extrapolative techniques (S-curve analysis, projections etc.); others need systematically explorative systems-based approaches. And some problems can only be solved by pure creativity and intuition. In practice, though, in most cases all types of methods are needed, as Chapter 3 illustrates.

It is easy to understand that every scenario analyst needs a well-equipped toolbox, no matter whether he or she is a manager or a professional analyst. It is almost always necessary to work on the problems from different angles and with different tools. Very simplistically, we can say that scenarios are based on three components where different skills are required:

- gathering information: intuition
- information analysis: logic
- modelling the future: creativity.

Gathering information requires intuition and the ability to see the broad picture, as well as powers of observation and a sense of detail. Above all else, the analysis requires logic and systematic thinking, but also the ability to see patterns and use intuition. Modelling requires an ability to think and draw conclusions, creativity and visualization.

The appendix describes a number of tools for information gathering, analysis and futures generation. Those methods can be divided in seven groups, based on their primary characteristics.

- media-based methods
- interview-based methods
- timeline-based methods
- generative, intuitive methods
- actor-oriented methods
- consequence-focused methods
- systems methods.

When we go through the other principles of scenario thinking we will briefly refer to different methods that could be used. You will find short descriptions of them in the appendix. First, however, we will give a short introduction to what we mean by the different terms.

Media-based methods

Media-based methods are methods where information is gathered from widely available sources, such as printed media, TV and, not least, the Internet, through which most sources (including most databases) are accessible. They can be used both for scanning and inspirational purposes, and for verifying information.

For scanning and inspirational purposes printed media are excellent. Walk into a well-equipped magazine store and you will realize how much you don't have a clue about. Browse through obscure magazines on topics you have never considered before, and I promise that you will find new ideas, get new perspectives and identify potential issues and trends you did not know about –

at least if you have an open mind. A number of famous trend analysts, including John Naisbitt and Faith Popcorn, have based a large part of their work on this type of media analysis.

The Internet and databases are better for verifying purposes and targeted searches. On the Internet there are also large amounts of free high-quality reports from major research institutes and consultancy firms.

Working with media as a source for trend-spotting and issues analysis requires an understanding of the dynamics of emerging issues. New issues are most often first identified in the communications of small, specialized communities, on web sites, in news groups and in specialized magazines (scientific or other). If you are looking for more mainstream issues, such as technologies, you should look in the more general, but still specialized media. There you will find 'the next big thing'. To bring an issue into prominence takes a social carrier, an event with high news value and, not least, a striking name. Then, you will be able to read about it everywhere.

Interview-based methods

Interview-based methods such as focus groups, expert panels, Delphi surveys (and of course interviews themselves) could be used for a range of purposes. First, they can be used to explore a topic and to generate hypotheses about central trends, key uncertainties and so on. Second, they can be used to clarify a certain topic or produce a more comprehensive picture of it. Third, they can be used to verify hypotheses about the future.

Timeline-based methods

Timeline analysis is a term that covers a number of quantitative and qualitative methods designed to identify patterns in time. Examples include time-series analysis, intuitive timeline drawing, historical analogies and pioneer analysis.

When you consider change over time, it is important to identify the general pattern. There are, in short, two general patterns: continuities and discontinuities. In the shorter timeframe most phenomena are perceived as continuities. However, the 'master chart' of history reveals that on the larger scale periods of continuity are usually followed by dramatic change and disruptions when external forces shake the kaleidoscope patterns and create new conditions for life over a relatively short period. That seems to be true for most systems, from geo-historical systems (the death of the dinosaurs and the rise of the mammals) and forests (which are 'restarted' by big fires), through civilizations (the Roman Empire, the British Empire) and industries (new technologies, new legislation etc.) to individuals (having kids, getting divorced etc.).

During the relatively stable periods we can identify three major patterns:

- *Invariances*. Invariances are constants. Some constants are linked to natural phenomena such as the sunrise and sunset, Newton's law, the human body's energy need and the like. Others are linked to human behaviours, such as humanity's constant expansion into new physical or intellectual territories. When searching for trends, we often miss central invariances.

- *Life cycles*. This is the general pattern for all living systems, including humans and even organizations. Children are born, grow up, get older and finally die. New products and markets generally also follow that pattern. Life cycles are made up of accelerated growth followed by a gradually decreasing growth rate.

- *Pure cycles*. The example above of sunrise and sunset could also be described as a pure cycle. Other examples are the economic cycles of various lengths (from 50–60 year Kondratieff cycles to short-term cycles of four or five years). In many cases, such as Kondratieff cycles, they are in fact the result of shifts in life cycles, where one socio-technological system is replaced by another.

We could also talk about a fourth type of pattern, namely *linear trends*. However, what we perceive as linear trends are generally segments of life cycles. For instance, we could view population growth as a linear trend, since we have a steady growth of some tens of millions every year. In reality there has been an accelerated growth that we may hope will shift to a retardation phase over the next decades.

The combination of continuities and discontinuities leads to a number of scenario patterns that could be recognized in society. Among them are the familiar Phoenix-scenarios (paradigm shift), The

Show Goes On (evolution), Everything's New (revolution), The Golden Days (growth peak), What Goes Around Comes Around (circular patterns), Winners and Losers, and Challenge and Response.

Generative, intuitive methods

The human mental bandwidth is limited. The psychologist George Miller took up the problem of mental limitation in 1956 in an article in the *Psychological Review* entitled 'The magical number seven, plus or minus two: some limits on our capacity for processing information'.

Miller concluded that there is evidence that in most situations we need to reduce the information complexity to around one byte, which is seven to eight bits or information units. We can do that through clustering or categorizing, but the reason we need to do so is that we do not have the capacity to memorize and handle large amounts of information consciously. Subconsciously, however, we have the capacity to process and handle much more information. While the brain can recognize or distinguish around 10 to 20 bits per second (before the information becomes pure noise) we can subconsciously receive billions of pieces of information.

One consequence of these facts is that we as human beings have huge reservoirs of subconscious wisdom that is waiting to be pulled out. And that is the basis of most creativity methods that have been developed over the last 20 years. Since analysis and criticism easily kills the creative and intuitive processes it is necessary to separate these phases. That is also what is needed in all scenario processes. The creativity expert Edward de Bono even suggests that we should put on different hats to express which mental mode we are in.

The necessary principle for productive creative thinking is simple:

- Divergent thinking first. That is, start with intuitive, creative or brainstorming activities, without restrictions.
- Convergent thinking later. Use convergent, analytical thinking to follow up, criticize, analyse, and deepen the material produced during the first phase.

Trust your guts. But not too much!

Actor-oriented methods

Much of what happens in our world, or within industries or organizations, is initiated by actors and springs out of the interplay between different actors and their specific goals.

To identify the actors, their goals, their strengths and alliances is the key to the understanding of the interplay on an arena. Specifically important are the customers, the competitors and, not least, potential new entrants and substitutes for the company's products and services. There are several methods to identify them. Scenarios could easily be drawn only on the basis of actor analysis.

Consequence-focused methods

To analyse potential consequences of activities, events, trends and other aspects is important. Through a careful, systematic consequence analysis, scenario writing becomes much easier. There are ways to analyse consequences, such as technology assessment, consequence trees and consequence matrixes among others.

Systems methods

Traditional cause–effect reasoning is not enough when we are dealing with such complex systems as society, complex topics, industries or organizations. To understand the interplay between different subsystems and change factors we need other types of analytical tools that can handle multivariate relationships.

Several methods can easily be utilized for scenario planning purposes, including cross-impact analysis, four-field analysis and causality analysis (loop diagrams). Dynamic simulation could also be a way to develop understanding of systems dynamics and to forecast system behaviour.

PRINCIPLE 2: HANDLE YOUR BRAIN WITH CARE

As we have seen, *Homo sapiens* is a scenario planning animal. Thinking in scenarios is what we constantly do. However, intuitive scenario thinking is somewhat different from the thinking that is needed to develop plausible scenarios. To do it, we need to force the brain to think in new directions and challenge old perceptions. But that requires energy, and thinking about the unfamiliar can even be exhausting. After a ten-hour workshop with demanding creative and analytical exercises most people are completely drained. It is costly for the brain to build new synapses, and thus we have a natural resistance to challenging perceptions. It is said that the brain consumes more energy during a difficult exam than during a marathon race. Thus, it is normally counterproductive to constantly challenge prejudices and perceptions. They should not be challenged until life is in danger.

Treating the brain with care, we should also be aware that it is by nature very selective in terms of what information it consciously extracts from the flood of data it receives. One reason for this is that memories are fragile. Facts need to be repeated to be remembered. Therefore the brain searches for information that can repair the memories and for information that confirms what we already know. And this is both a conscious and a subconscious process. Furthermore, the more knowledge we have within a certain area, the more energy and time we need merely to keep that knowledge updated. Consequently, we will have less interest and capacity to search for challenging or diverging information.

The brain is an imaginative organ. We think in images, music, senses, feelings, but not in abstract entities such as 'not', 'more than' and the like. For instance, negations do not exist in the mind, and do not exist in the real world either. Therefore, images and vivid language and descriptions, such as stories, tales and narratives are powerful communication tools. Great communicators have known that since the beginning of history.

Different types of images of the future tend to affect us differently.[18] In the combat between positive and negative images, or threats, the negative takes the lead. And in the battle between near and distant futures, the near ones win. Consequently, most people have a tendency to emphasize imminent threats, rather than distant opportunities. This is usually a successful survival strategy, but not always. And it is good to be aware of the brain's general tendency to neglect or over-emphasize certain information, moods of thinking and futures.

Another example of the brain's function as both helper and hindrance is the limited bandwidth of the mental capacity. Although we can subconsciously receive large amounts of information, the conscious capacity to handle them is very limited. Therefore we need to reduce complexity in order to cope with it. And we need to do this not only intuitively, but also with more systematic methods that help us to do it step by step.

PRINCIPLE 3: THINK IN DRAMAS

'Scenario' is a term that originates in the theatre; a scenario is a brief description of the course of events in a play. Fundamentally, scenario thinking means viewing the world (or the industry) as a great drama with various more or less controllable forces and a number of players trying to influence the plot for their own goals and intentions.

In the theatre or film context a scenario should be a brief but full description. That means that a scenario is not a snapshot of the 'end' of the film but a description of events. If we transfer this concept to futures thinking it would mean that a complete scenario should describe developments from now until a given time (rather than being a mere snapshot of the future). It must be consistent, not full of inner contradictions.

With the drama perspective, at each point in time the scenario should give a description of:

- the players: the principal persons who are moving the action forward (WHO?)
- the events: what is happening (WHAT?)
- the time when it is happening (WHEN?)
- the scene where the events are taking place (WHERE?)
- props: what props are needed and in what way are the actions carried out (HOW?)
- motives: why is this happening (WHY?).

Briefly, we can say the scenario should answer the questions: Who is doing what? When? Where? How (together with whom)? And why?

Scenario descriptions usually lack one or more of the above dimensions. Most commonly, motives and players are left out, which means an indeterminate 'it' with obscure purposes is controlling developments.

Thinking in scenarios like this means seeing the future as a drama or play that has not yet been staged. It is the future as a theatrical forum, where anyone can step onto the stage and improvise a script.

PRINCIPLE 4: THINK IN FUTURES

The essence of scenario planning is thinking in futures. In order to be a good scenario thinker it is necessary to develop the capability to think in terms of futures.

Some people are natural futures thinkers. They constantly think in terms of 'where will that lead', 'what is this a sign of' and so on. As soon as they recognize a new phenomenon they start to speculate on far-reaching consequences. Such people are often imaginative, receptive and image-thinking personalities. They are born futures thinkers. But in fact most people can improve their futures thinking capability with the help of a few techniques and some training.

There are numbers of ways that futures thinking can be improved. We have previously said that futures, or scenarios, can be created through a 'from present to future' perspective or a 'from future to present' one. The first approach builds on causality thinking. From events or trends in the present you can generate consequences and build consequence trees or causality maps. This kind of thinking is more analytical by nature than the 'future to present' approach, which is more creative. First you have to imagine the future state, and from that point develop a 'history of the future', either through a mainly creative process or through a more analytical approach where you create the path from the future backwards step by step.

Most people are able to use both methods, although they prefer one of them. The easiest way to improve one's ability to think in futures is to start writing letters from the future, where you describe to some old friend what the world is like, how business is going or whatever else you care to write about. You can write visions (as in the examples in Chapter 3), or normative scenarios in this way, but you can also write any type of scenario by using this simple technique as a starting point. If the scenario is to be used for planning purposes it needs to be tested for consistency, plausibility and similar aspects, but that is a question for later.

Another way to get started is to start to write down future events, things that might happen in the future. These statements could then be sorted or clustered and could be a starting point for scenario writing. One way to develop simple statements of the future is to make posters or futures articles with headlines and introductions that describe future states. All creative methods that could help futures thinking are useful.

The most powerful question to improve futures thinking is still 'What if . . .?'

Methods

Some of the methods briefly described in the appendix that could be used to develop futures thinking are:

Trend extrapolation: This is useful in the present-to-future mode. Identify present trends and extrapolate them into the future.

Media scanning: To scan media is a powerful way to identify trends (or generate hypotheses) and to stimulate creativity, bring in new perspectives and ideas.

Guruing: By guruing we simply mean asking experts for their opinions of the future.

Delphi surveys: Delphi surveys are a more systematic way to collect expert opinions about the future. Experts are asked to give specific opinions on when or with what certainty a certain event will occur.

Future history: To write future histories is a powerful way to create imaginative scenarios. The backward look also stimulates creativity, makes it easier to identify possible future events, actors' moves and so on. It is less wearying than more analytical approaches. The brain likes to have fun, and writing futures histories is usually fun.

Headlines and poster production: Similar to futures histories, but instead of writing letters or a history of the future, you make snapshots in the form of posters, headlines and short articles.

Intuitive timelines and statistical time series: Timelines can be drawn intuitively but can also be computed through statistical methods based on historical data. The first method is usually an effective way to clarify own ideas about future courses.

Event production: To think in terms of future events is a good starting point for a more thorough analysis. Future events are also necessary to turn a limited futures plot into a vivid scenario description.

PRINCIPLE 5: THINK IN UNCERTAINTY

To manage uncertainty has been considered the key managerial task. And scenario planning is a methodology designed to handle uncertainty.

There are often several reasons why a decision environment is perceived as uncertain. In its most simple form uncertainty derives from lack of information or lack of analysis and thinking. In such cases uncertainty can be reduced by simple intelligence and it is possible to make forecasts good enough to base decisions on. Alternative scenarios are not even needed for such decision making.

A second type of uncertainty, where scenario techniques are useful, is the case of dichotomous or discrete uncertainties. Those are characterized by the 'either–or'. Either we get this situation or we get that. Either the UK joins the Euro – or not. Sometimes there are more than two possible outcomes, but there is always a discrete number of futures that the organization has to handle. With this type of uncertainty you are sometimes able to build roadmaps and link probabilities to each alternative in each conjunction, and thereby may hope to get an impression of the overall probability of each scenario.

Most commonly, though, the uncertainty is caused by the speed of change or by great complexity, or both. At moderate to high levels of complexity and speed, linear change dominates and it is meaningful to talk about an uncertainty space. It is still possible to identify certain trends, to sort out the probable overall direction and to identify a limited number of uncertainty dimensions that could be used to reduce the uncertainty to a manageable number of scenarios.

At even higher levels of uncertainty we end up in an area of genuine uncertainty where non-linear, discontinuous change dominates. At that level scenario planning is no longer relevant. Instead you need to apply techniques for pattern recognition and work with analogies. This type of uncertainty is often present when we analyse very immature and turbulent markets.

Fruitful strategic actions differ at different levels of uncertainty. The purpose of a strategic move is either to preserve one's options to play, that is to cope with the changes, or to influence the future trajectory and thus to take the lead in the future. The first strategic posture could be called reactive and the second shaping.

However, it is worth remembering that complex systems can never be fully controlled, as every manager, school teacher or even parent very well knows. To be able to control a complex system you need to be equally complex as a controller, as Ashby's law of requisite variety states. What you can do though, is intervene in the system, introduce noise that changes the trajectory. This kind of noise may be new information, new products, new standards or new strategies. An example is the noise (or maybe voice) interference so successfully used as a strategy by Alan Greenspan for over a decade. Big players in immature markets that have not developed standards can also use the strategy of standard interference. Introducing a new standard that the major players will accept reduces uncertainty, and the architect of the standard will automatically acquire a leading position in the market. The more uncertain the system is, the more powerful this kind of uncertainty reduction will be.

Methods

Analogies: To use historical or other analogies is often a fruitful method when we are dealing with non-linear change at high level of uncertainty, for instance within emerging markets or industries. What other industries have gone through something similar? Has this happened before? What similarities are there between the early 2000s and the early 1930s? If this is an animal, what animal is it? And what is it becoming?

Complexity plotting and uncertainty analysis: Trying to identify the complexity and speed in different segments of the business environment is often a good starting point for analysis.

PRINCIPLE 6: THINK IN SYSTEMS

Problems that are created by our current level of thinking can't be solved by that same level of thinking.

(Albert Einstein)

Over and over again throughout this book, we have talked about systems. And systems thinking is really the core of scenario thinking. Systems thinking is about thinking in levels of change, in dependencies and interdependencies. Over the last decades systems thinking has become part of every manager's, and almost every individual's, framework. Nevertheless, it is worth describing some of the applications of systems thinking in the context of scenario development.

Albert Einstein talks about the impossibility of solving new problems with old thinking. Scholars in the field of organizational learning refer to that as the need for double-loop learning.[19] The idea of double-loop learning is that in order to learn people and organizations need to climb up to the next level, view their practices from outside in and reflect on them. That is the only way to fundamentally change patterns of behaviour, and that is also what Einstein talks about. What that fundamentally implies is that systems can never be understood from the inside. They need to be viewed from outside. Consequently, for instance, an industry can never be understood or changed only from within. It must be explained and renewed from outside too.

In his book *The Meaning of the Twentieth Century* (1964), the economist Kenneth Boulding developed the concept of systems levels. Boulding identified seven levels of open living systems and made a number of other contributions to systems thinking (Table 4.1). According to the systems view there is a systems-within-systems perspective that is the key to understanding every system. For instance, what happens on the organizational level affects groups within the organization, and vice versa.

From a scenario planning perspective Levels 5 to 7 in Boulding's model are the relevant ones. However, as we also consider

Table 4.1. Boulding's seven levels of open living systems

Level 1	Cell	The basic unit of life
Level 2	Organ	The organic system within bodies
Level 3	Organism	Single organisms such as humans, animals, etc.
Level 4	Group	Teams, departments, families and similar member-based bodies
Level 5	Organization	Companies, community, private and public organizations
Level 6	Society	States, countries, nations, regions within nations
Level 7	Supranational systems	Global systems, continents, international regions, Earth

individual stakeholders, action groups and the like, Levels 3 and 4 are sometimes relevant too.

If we consider the context of a specific decision, we can see that there are system levels above and beneath the actual decision. External to a corporation there are at least two relevant levels of environment. On the higher level, there is the parallel to Boulding's supranational system, which in the case of business means the general business environment described by macroeconomic, ecological, demographic, technological, political, social and legislative changes that have an impact on all subsystems. Closer to the organization we find the immediate business environment, the business arena, which is the parallel to society in Boulding's model. This is the community of organizations and stakeholders that collaborate and compete and that together define the industry or branch of industry. This second system could in turn be divided into subsystems. (See Figure 4.1.)

What goes on inside the organization could also be described as part of the strategic corporate business context. Decisions and moves made at any level from single individuals to groups, divisions or subsidiaries are usually relevant to strategic decisions.

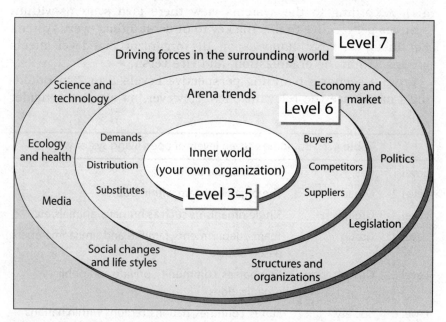

Figure 4.1. Model of the organizational business context and its parallel to Boulding's systems model

If the aim of the scenario process is to guide strategic decisions for a business unit within a larger corporation, for instance, the corporate level becomes part of the external business environment. The decision could be described as being made on Level 4 in Boulding's model, or on a lower part of Level 5.

Systems of trends

Systems thinking is also central to the framing of trends and changes. The iceberg is a common metaphor used to describe the relationship between single events, trends and drivers (Figure 4.2).[20] What we actually see, when we scan the business or general environment for new trends are single events or phenomena. Series of events could be structured in patterns or, in futures language, trends. In terms of systems, trends are on higher levels than single events. Trends can be linked to other trends, and may be driven by other trends or clusters of trends (structures). To be able to identify the structures that drive a system, and thus are the key elements in a scenario plot, you need to get beneath the surface and identify the general patterns and structures behind visible events in the present. And in order to

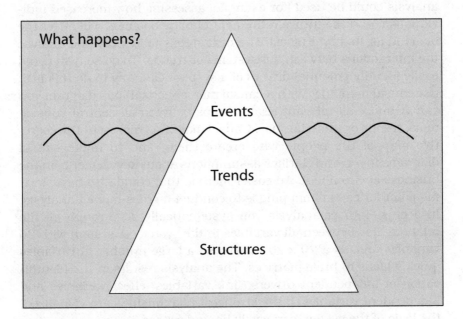

Figure 4.2. The iceberg metaphor: structural changes are driving systems at lower levels and are eventually observed as events and actions

generate a scenario plot and write a vivid scenario story you need to get back to the surface again to develop the scenario logic (plot) and 'dress' the incomplete plot with clarifying events and actions.

It is sometimes said that strategy is about asking 'Why?' over and over again until you get to the root causes. Taking the iceberg metaphor, this is similar to diving below the surface of the sea.

The process of writing scenarios is consequently a journey from the particular and specific to the general and structural, and back to the specific again. From low system levels, to high system levels, and back to the low levels again. This kind of journey is also the general pattern of the planning cycle, and very similar to the earlier statement by Albert Einstein. Problems, questions and challenges are generally generated in very concrete and specific ways: that is, on the operational level. Often the problems transmute into tactical questions regarding operations, human resources and the like, which in turn have a tendency to become strategic questions before they can be rerouted to the tactical and finally the operational level again.

There are several tools that could be used to clarify systems logic in scenario planning. To analyse systems (or trends) that impact on other systems at the same, lower or higher levels, trend-impact analysis could be used (for example, assessing how increased individualism and the future retirement of baby boomers will affect the demand for luxury cruises). The next step is to identify and analyse the interactions between subsystems or trends. To do so, you could easily identify potential drivers of a system. One way to do this is to use causal mapping. With a causal map or causal-loop diagram you can visualize all relevant relationships between all central subsystems, trends or uncertainties. Causal diagrams represent the cognitive map of the people who create them, and to make causal diagrams in a group clarifies assumptions about key elements in the business environment. An easier method that could also be a starting point for causal mapping is to conduct a cross-impact analysis. In a cross-impact analysis you systematically go through all the relationships between all variables in the system. A system with 20 variables creates a 20×20 matrix, so a large number of variables quickly leads to huge matrices. The analysis results in the identification of independent drivers, link variables, effect variables and independent variables. If the strongest relationships are visualized, the logic of the system can easily be understood.

Key to all systems analysis is the choice of a relevant descriptive level. If you generalize too much, most of the information will get lost in a general 'noise'. If on the other hand you are too specific in your description, you will end up with endless amounts of trends, factors and so on and will need to cluster your variables in order to be able to use them. The general advice is that to be a good systems thinker you will have to be able to shift between the specific and the general and to transform the general into specific conclusions and vice versa.

Methods

SIM (single-impact analysis): Single-impact analysis is a general method of codifying simple cause–effect links in the format of a matrix. Each effect is given a number based on the level of impact.

Consequence tree: A consequence tree is a more visual way of identifying effects of single trends. The trend is depicted by the trunk of the tree. Drivers are located in the root system and the possible effects are shown as branches and twigs.

CIM (cross-impact analysis): CIM is another semi-quantitative method where interrelations between different subsystems are analysed in a matrix, rather than simple cause–effect relationships. The output is a systems description identifying the drivers of the system.

Causal mapping: Causal mapping or a causal-loop diagram is a formal format for describing the relations between different entities (variables) in a system. A positive relationship (in which an increase in A causes an increase in B) is represented by a plus arrow. Similarly a negative relationship (increase in A causes decrease in B) is shown by a minus arrow.

Systems modelling: Systems modelling is based on the transformation of causal maps into mathematical representation that can be simulated.

PRINCIPLE 7: THINK IN ACTORS AND MOVES

The future of for instance a certain sector of industry, a business arena, will not just emerge. It will be shaped, both by forces out of reach for the industry actors, and also by the players within the arena. Their needs, intentions, strategic moves and alliances will be of great importance for the future of the industry sector. The strategic moves taken by your own organization as well as by other players will determine the future.

Rolf Jensen, former director of the Copenhagen Institute for Future Studies, discusses what he calls 'The Call' and 'The Holy Grail' of the organization.[21] The call is the wakeup summons that rouses the organization from its bed, willing to go out in the world and fight the struggle to win The Holy Grail. The Call could be described as the organization's 'pain', the energizing problems that must be solved and that drive the organization out of its secure corner. The Call pushes the organization outwards, forwards. The Holy Grail is the desired vision that pulls the organization on, that strengthens it for the demanding journey forward.

In more prosaic terms the Call is the organization's challenges and the Grail is the vision. The greater the challenge and the stronger the vision, the more probable it is that the organization will do something, that it will make strategic moves.

The ability to make proper strategic moves, and to succeed with those strategies, depends on the strengths and weaknesses of the organization. How well is it prepared for the fight with the dragons and gate-keepers of the Grail? Can the organization leverage capabilities through alliances? Are there shared goals with other actors? What kind of blocks and alliances can be expected?

By mapping all the present and potential actors in the arena, and by tracking their past moves, we quickly get a deeper understanding of the interplay between different actors: which trends, subsystems and issues they may affect and what potential moves they may make. In fact, actors can be treated in a very similar way to other 'system elements' such as trends and events. And they can be analysed with similar methods. For instance, cross-impact matrices could be used to study the interplay among different actors and trends, or among either actors or trends.

By analysing the possible moves of single actors or groups, scenarios can be developed directly from the actor analysis.

Applying actor thinking inside–out leads to the perspective of strategic moves. Changes in the competitive landscape, especially non-linear change, generate threats as well as opportunities. The more old structures erode, the greater the opportunities to change the rule of the games. But on the other hand, with increased uncertainty come increasing risks. Applying the actor perspective to one's own organization is, from the scenario perspective, the link between future and strategy: between the exploration of possible and plausible futures, and the creation of the desired future!

Methods

Actor/stakeholder analysis: Actor analysis is a fundamental method where actors are plotted together with key characteristics as goals, means, strengths and weaknesses.

Value-chain analysis: Value-chain analysis is useful as a means to analyse a business area and its key actors.

Competitor analysis: Competitor analysis is a version of actor analysis where competitors' goals, strengths, weaknesses, alliances and historical and possible strategic moves are analysed.

The Principles of Strategic Thinking

Scenario thinking is by nature strategic, in the sense that it deals with the big picture. Therefore all that has been said earlier about the principles behind scenario thinking is applicable also to strategic thinking. But moving from scenarios – that is, pictures of the business context – to strategies requires something more. And that something has to do with the processes going on inside the organization, and the organization's links to the external world.

A list of principles of strategic thinking could be very extensive. However, we have decided to cut it down to a minimum of principles that are the most relevant for strategy in terms of scenario planning. Thus, we have reduced them to the 'magical number seven': the most holy of all holy numbers (the seven days of the week, the seven deadly sins, the seven notes of the musical scale, the seven wonders of the world, the seven primary colours etc.).

PRINCIPLE 1: THINK IN PARADOXES

The world is full of paradoxes, and always has been. And so is the business world. Strategic management is essentially the art of managing paradoxes: growth and profitability; innovation and efficiency.

One of the great pitfalls for managers is to neglect the existence of paradoxes, or at least to underestimate the need for paradox management. Professor Henry Mintzberg recently pointed out this mistake in an article on the art and evolution of strategic management. He noted that managers as well as consultants tend to focus on one aspect of strategic management, while neglecting the others:

> Consultants have been like big game hunters embarking on their safaris for tusk and trophies, while academics have preferred

photo safaris – keeping a safe distance from the animals they pretend to observe. Managers take one narrow perspective or another – the glories of planning or the wonders of learning, the demands of external competitive analyses or the imperatives of an internal 'resource-based' view. Much of this writing and advising has been decidedly dysfunctional, simply because managers have no choice but to cope with the entire beast.

(Mintzberg and Lampel 1999: 21)

We have, throughout this book pointed at the need for 'both–and' perspectives. Let us briefly repeat some of the most relevant in the context of scenario planning. We will come back to some of them later on.

History and future: Good strategies must be rooted in the organization's history, tradition, competence and culture – but must at the same time be designed to cope with and to challenge the future, far reaching enough to generate the necessary energy.

Continuity and change: Good strategies, even in times of turmoil, must consist of elements of continuity combined with enough elements of change to enable the organization to undertake necessary moves.

Structure and flexibility: The organizational structure must be loose enough to let things happen, and tight enough to make them happen.

Principles and rule-breaking: To get the necessary stability one has to develop some non-negotiable principles of communication, core strategies, organizational structure and so on, but on the other hand rule-breaking behaviour has to be encouraged in order to cultivate a thinking and playing culture.

Variation and simplicity: To cope with a complex world you need to have a broad repertoire. On the other hand, to build quality you need to emphasize a few specific factors, build your strategy around a few well-defined principles.

Experimentation and concentration: In raplex environments one has to experiment and search one's way into the future. But to get momentum one has to concentrate on a few carefully selected areas.

PRINCIPLE 2: THINK IN VISIONS

Fast-growing companies exist in every industry, in boom times and in bust, and are distinguished from more ordinary companies by having different reference points. While the fast grower considers a yearly growth rate of 25 per cent natural, for others 5–10 per cent is excellent. Fast growers expect higher growth levels.

Visions occur in different forms and under different names throughout history. In almost every social science visions (in different terms) are seen as essential for humans as well as organizations and societies. From modern sports psychology we are all aware of the consequences of 'bad thinking'. What separates the winners from the ordinary is not so much the muscle as the mind. When golf player Annika Sörenstam set a new standard in women's golf it was based on new thinking, new reference points. 'Why use four strikes in this par four lane when you could do it in three,' she thought, and set out for bogeys.

Strategy researchers Fiegenbaum, Hart and Schendel (1996) propose that what is true for individuals also works on the organizational level. Just like individuals, organizations need constantly moving reference points to keep pace with the changing business environment.

In Table 5.1 their conclusions, based on literature research, are presented. To summarize, they found that organizational

Table 5.1. Strategic choice behaviour according to Fiegenbaum *et al.*

	Above reference point	Below reference point
Perception of new issues	Threat	Opportunity
	Sitting on top of the world	At the bottom looking up
	Potential loss	Potential gain
	Negative	Positive
Organizational processes	Constricted	Open
	Rigid	Flexible
Nature of response or behaviour	Risk-averse	Risk-taking
	Conservative	Daring
	Defensive	Offensive

behaviour changes as organizations move beyond their reference points, or in other words, when they surpass their goals or visions. Below this reference point the organization is 'up and coming'; above it, it behaves as a defender of past success. Thus, we need to think in visions, and to rethink the visions constantly – not only as individuals, but also as organizations.

History is full of excellent vision-driven organizations, and individuals, that moved beyond their own reference points – into mediocrity and failure. Without moving reference points, you might be one of them.

PRINCIPLE 3: THINK IN JAMMING

In Chapter 1 we concluded that the main challenge to business leaders today is to craft robust hard-to-copy business concepts and strategies, without neglecting the need for responsiveness. We also concluded that jamming is a superb metaphor for the organizational behaviour needed.

Jamming is based on that combination of a few guiding principles, such as a steady beat, combined with improvisation and pragmatism. Thinking in jamming means sorting out what can be controlled from what cannot. It means an emphasis on flexibility that is necessary for future success, and stability that provides the backbone of the organization. For instance, it is generally more important to control language, values and patterns of communication (that is, the culture) than to control individuals' actions.

In organizational terms jamming means 'patching'. Patching is dividing the organization into logically internally consistent units, controlling the language and rules of inter-patch communication, and then letting the organization play.

In terms of strategic moves and actions, jamming means getting the broad picture right and getting mentally prepared for the actions – and acting in an improvisational way, based on the broad picture.

Jamming could also be applied as a guiding principle in workshops and project groups. During such processes it is necessary to define the rules, pick the tune, decide who keeps the pace (plays the bass) and so on.

PRINCIPLE 4: THINK IN TIME

Thinking in time is related to thinking in jamming. The jamming approach is very much time-based, and time is becoming an increasingly important strategic issue. Global consumer goods companies like Nokia often only get one chance to put a new product on the market. If the introduction fails there will be no second chance; the life cycle is just too short. *Timing* thus becomes a critical issue.

But thinking in time is not only about timing. Time is also about *pace*. What companies like Nokia and Intel do is to use time as a strategic weapon. Shona Brown and Kathleen Eisenhardt noticed in *Competing on the Edge* (1997) that Intel control their market through their 18-month cycle. By introducing a new generation of chips every 18 months, they set the pace for a whole industry. Other companies, like 3M, use time pacing as an organizational principle to press for innovation. By demanding that a certain proportion of sales from each business unit should come from products not more than three years old, for instance, the corporate management stimulates innovation in the whole company.

To use time pacing as a strategic weapon, companies need to deliver *on time*. Companies with internally structured processes and the ability to be on time also tend to perform much better than those that constantly miss their deadlines.[22]

A fourth central aspect of time is *speed*, and specifically speed of innovation. There are thousands of tons of literature on innovation and innovation processes. Innovation in terms of products and markets can be seen as a process that combines systematic recombination and spontaneous innovation. The biological parallels to those two activities are DNA recombination and mutation. Mutation occurs as a spontaneous or enforced process where the genetic material is recoded. Recombination (producing hybrid DNA) means that new genetic material is purposefully added to an existing gene pool. With hybrid-DNA techniques the genetic innovation process has been boosted considerably, and things that were once impossible can now be done as standard procedures. When existing products, markets and business concepts are viewed with the eyes of the genetic engineer, existing innovation processes can be improved in terms of speed and accuracy.

PRINCIPLE 5: THINK IN RESOURCES

During the 1990s the research-based perspective, in different flavours, became a dominating perspective in strategy. To think in resources, competences and hard-to-copy core competences became standard procedures in most organizations.

As we discussed in Chapter 3, thinking in resources is fundamental in strategy, and every strategy must match existing resources. But thinking in resources is not only to think of 'what we have' and 'what we need'. It also needs inertia thinking and leverage thinking.

As organizations grow up and mature, they develop specific behaviours, skills and traditions as responses to organizational challenges. They collect and aggregate the tangible and intangible resources needed for the specific time and place. As time passes and the organization faces new challenges, some of those earlier strengths become weaknesses, barriers to the way forward. From real resources they become organizational inertia, dead or dysfunctional ideas, material or behaviours. Thinking in resources demands that we consider such negative resources too. Sometimes inertia can be transformed into relevant strengths, but not always. Sometimes the old barrels are not good enough and need to be replaced.

Small resources can often be leveraged through skilful thinking and acting. There are a number of principles for leveraging resources. Concentration is one, spatially or in terms of focus. Spatial concentration means that dispersed resources are gathered into one place; it is often a fruitful strategy when it comes to getting more out of research departments or knowledge workers. Concentration of resources on specific goals is another strategy that is often successful.

Accumulation of resources is another strategy, and requires that knowledge and behaviours be codified and 'saved'. Resources could also be leveraged by borrowing strengths from others, partner companies, suppliers or customers. Complementing this is yet another leverage strategy which means that you simply add what is missing, following the rule of synergy that 1+1>2. Recombination of resources in new ways is also a commonly used leverage strategy, though unfortunately not always practised skilfully. Conserving and recovering resources are yet more leverage strategies.

But essentially, what thinking in resources is all about is viewing and treating the company *and its context* as a resource pool.

PRINCIPLE 6: THINK IN LIFE CYCLES

Basic technologies, as well as products, markets and even organizations follow patterns that could be described as life cycles. We have previously said that scenario planning is specifically useful in the turbulent periods characterized by new technology or business concepts.

The life cycle perspective is applicable in a number of situations and central to the understanding of the challenges that organizations face. In immature markets (as well as organizations) market leaders must enforce stability through strategic moves that make followers fall into line. Managers must similarly create an organizational structure that can function as a backbone in the growing body. During the stable growth period the challenges are linked to the exploitation of a growing potential, and during the mature stagnation period the market challenge is cost efficiency and a smooth exit. From the organizational perspective, however, the challenge is usually bigger. At that point the people and organization have to prepare for the great leap to the next wave. Old paradigms need to be de-programmed and old habits need to be changed.

The growth curve or life cycle can also be used as an evaluation tool. Map your projects, products, technologies or new ideas on the curve to find out which one is where, and what to do with them. Which products have their future behind them, and which have the future ahead? The analysis will not give a complete answer, but adds one more piece to the jigsaw puzzle.

PRINCIPLE 7: THINK IN EXPERIMENTS AND BETS

Imagine a misty mountain landscape. You are leading your troops forward, upward, but you do not know exactly where you are. Your task is to climb the highest peak, but you do not even know whether you are on the right mountain. What do you do? The only way to handle the situation is to send out scouts – in different directions – and hope that some of them find the right mountain to climb.

This mountaineering challenge is what companies in immature markets face. It is also an illustration of what the future is largely about. The greater the speed and uncertainty, the more misty and mountainous the landscape becomes.

The scouting activity is similar to testing the future out. In terms of product or market development it could be described as low-cost experimentation. The military commander bets on different directions and sends out the scouts, hoping that some of them will get back in one way or another. But a good general does not risk the whole force.

Putting this image in terms of business strategies, the leader handles the future as a portfolio of options, projects or experimental projects. Leaders bet on different scenarios or even different concepts. But, once again, they do it without endangering the key elements. With this slightly conservative risk-sharing strategy they can slowly feel their way into the future. Whenever they find a promising road, they can raise their bets. That is thinking in experiments and bets.

Appendix 1: Methods

MEDIA-BASED METHODS

Media scanning

Media scanning is a simple and popular method either for continuous monitoring or for an occasional overview or inspiration as a part of a scenario planning process. A simple media scan can often be a good complement to brainstorming around key factors that have an impact on the focal area of concern.

It is easy to create a simple system for media scanning. Make it a practice to regularly tear out articles from the press that seems relevant for the areas you study. If you watch a feature on TV or listen to something on the radio, it is easiest to note down details on a piece of paper. If you find something on the Internet it is simplest to copy it to your computer or make a print-out.

All this information is accumulated and regularly classified and assorted around proper themes. At regular intervals you go through the piles and summarize the observations.

When you scan a great number of papers it is important to do it quickly, just a couple of minutes per paper. It is also important to have a couple of hypotheses in mind and look for material that either confirms or contradicts them. It is also important to keep an eye out for other phenomena that seem to show something new. New phenomena can be embryos of tomorrow's big issues. (See also the section on issues management.)

Trend-tracker groups

A good way to engage people in the watching process is through organizing a small trend-tracker group within the company or department. The members of the group can monitor either the same or different issues. Elect a coordinator whose main task will be to collect and sort out the material. At intervals the group meets to analyse parts of the collected material. The group should have access to the collected information in advance.

Media watch

There are many companies that offer different types of media watch, particularly of the press and Internet, but also radio and TV. Often the results are distributed on intranet portals. Most big companies and organizations utilize this kind of service. Most often the watch concerns features about the company, its products and competitors. If you want to look for new phenomena or a broader question, though, it is difficult to farm it out to external watchers.

Keyword analysis

When you have observed a phenomenon or an issue, you often consciously or subconsciously start to formulate hypotheses. Imagine that you work in the human resource field and have noticed an increased level of discussion on leadership in virtual organizations. A number of articles have addressed this issue. It is not unlikely that this is a new phenomenon and that interest in it has increased strongly over the last year. You can test this hypothesis with database searches on different keywords that describe this type of leadership and organization. When did the issues first occur? When did researchers begin to talk about them? When did they become widespread? Database searches can give good answers to these kinds of questions.

Content analysis

A keyword search is a quick and effective way to get an overview of changes over time. A more time-consuming way is to analyse and codify the content of articles. Content analysis is a recognized method that was frequently used during the Second World War. Lately the technique has become commonly known through the work of the futurist John Naisbitt.

Content analysis is built on the following presumptions:

- Material that is put out for one purpose often carries other implicit messages. These are often more authentic than the ones that are directly communicated.
- Implicit information can be identified, codified, analysed and interpreted. There are patterns in the information that describe the present state of affairs and reveal trends and attitudes.

- Content analysis can very often correct, mirror and test information from other sources.

To carry out content analysis oneself using a lot of information is expensive and time-consuming.

INTERVIEW-BASED METHODS

Delphi surveys

The Delphi method was invented in the 1960s and got its name from the oracle of Delphi. The original purpose of Delphi surveys was to obtain quantitative future assessments by letting experts judge different statements. The method has most often been used for technological forecasting.

A Delphi survey is carried out as follows:

1. Formulate a question with quantitative answers (When? How many per cent?).
2. Ask the respondents privately by telephone, face-to-face or questionnaire.
3. Compile the results and calculate a median value.
4. Bring back the results to the respondents and ask for new responses.
5. Compile the final results. (If necessary one can do another round before the final result is compiled.)

One of the weaknesses of the Delphi method in its original form is that it aims at getting a common opinion when there perhaps is no consensus; different opinions may be hidden by a compilation that gives a mean or averaged result. Today the method is applied less stringently, and Delphi has become a general name for different kinds of interview-based methods where the respondents are asked to assess future prospects.

Delphic conversation: structured interviews

Delphic conversation is a more open form of Delphi that does not aim to produce quantitative results. The structured inter-views can of course be quantified according to the questions that the respondents themselves raise or the answers they give, but this is a different kind of quantifying from the one described above.

Opinion polls

An opinion is the perception a group has of a certain issue: for example the general public's view of nuclear power or a client's perception of the company's service. Opinion polls can be used for two different purposes: to obtain a quantitative picture of the state of the art right now, or to monitor changes over time, for example changes of opinions or the growth of new phenomena.

Long-range data

To obtain a palpable picture of changes over time it is necessary to use long-range data collected over a long time span, from a couple of months to many decades. In order to compare answers from one survey to another, it is necessary that questions are put in the same context, since the answers people give to specific questions are affected by the context in which they are put. If you ask a question about the importance of the environment in a questionnaire that focuses on work and leisure, for example, you will get an answer that is more positive than if you put it in one concerning unemployment and poverty.

When working on changed opinions and attitudes it is important to know that:

- There are greater differences on every given occasion between different groups within the same generation than between different generations
- As opinions change, practically all demographic groups in the society change in the same direction. The consequence is that the differences between groups at a given measuring point are almost always less than differences within any single group at two different measuring points with a number of years in between.

Focus groups

Qualitative research, and above all focus groups, have recently been gaining ground. In a focus group a number of people meet for a couple of hours to discuss one or two specific questions. These groups are often used when you want to get a picture of how customers or potential customers think of their future needs. The focus group originates from conversational therapy and has become very popular lately. The foremost reason is the visual simplicity of the method. It is simple for decision makers to get an understanding of the demands and wishes of the target group. On top of that, a series of three or four focus groups is much cheaper to conduct than a bigger quantitative survey. Focus groups are good for identifying questions, for testing a hypothesis and for going deeper into interesting answers in quantitative studies. It is, however, not an instrument that can be used to confirm the accuracy of a hypothesis.

Expert panels

Many companies acquire expert panels they can refer to regularly. A panel of experts will often have the role of strategic advisors who are consulted before strategic decisions. We can distinguish two different groups of experts: first, there are experts on the focal issues, and second there are customers and consumers. In scenario processes, it is often fruitful to bring such panels in as idea generators and scenario evaluators. More and more organizations have expert panels that they consult regularly. The advantages are that the participants get to know the organization, and the panels are easy to administer as the same groups are used all the time and there is no need for new selections.

Guruing

We come across gurus every day. TV loves them. We run into the same phenomena at conferences; they want people who can present a message that seems immediately convincing or who by virtue of their position can give weight to their words. An alternative to guruing is to listen to people in your network. For this, it is important to gather a network of people with true integrity who dare to express their opinions even if they are not popular. It is of particular importance to bring in people with a good sense of what is happening in society. Artists, young people, people from industries where there are lots of changes going on, people with lots of contacts, and above all people that you normally don't meet.

Executive panels

An executive panel is a variant of the expert panel. In an executive panel, managers and other co-workers in leading positions come together. They form an internal expert panel. A variation of this is holding internal youth panels in order to get hold of the perspectives of the young co-workers. Some companies have even constituted a juvenile board.

Creative future groups

A creative future group is a problem-solving group that can be either internal or external, or a mix of the two. What separates the creative future group from a group of experts, a focus group or the other types mentioned is that here the members are active as problem solvers. By using creative future groups the expert study is transformed into a participatory scenario planning exercise. The ideal number of participants is seven or eight people. That is large enough to obtain a variety of perspectives, but small enough for creative discussions that are not distracted by formal meeting rituals.

The creative future group focuses firmly on well-defined questions and their work is based on a previously given working method. A theme for a gathering may be to identify trends or key factors that will affect the development of the area under study, or to identify consequences of alternative scenarios. There are three basic criteria for a good functioning of a creative future group:

- All opinions are valued as equally important.
- There is a clear question for the meeting and a method to cope with it.
- A process leader keeps the group together and guides it forward.

Future dialogue

Future dialogue is a seminar method that makes it possible to handle a great number of parallel future groups within the framework of a single seminar. It is possible to have more than a hundred participants in a future dialogue.

During a future dialogue conference people work their way through a series of questions, for example: 'Which are the most important trends that have an impact on our industry?' on to 'What will we do when we get home?' The work is done in groups that at the start are as mixed as possible. By the time they approach the tangible proposals they consist of people who work near to each other in their everyday operations. Continuously changing group members ensures that all questions will be raised and nothing will be overlooked. A question that is raised by one person in the first round can, by the end of the conference, be imbued with the thinking of all the groups.

There are always short presentations on slides that are copied and distributed to the groups between the sessions. A short introduction is also given before each session. The leaders of the conference can collate the results of every step during the sessions, and provide all the participants with complete documentation before they leave. A future dialogue normally lasts from lunchtime until lunch the next day.

Participatory future studies

A participatory future study is a model to conduct future studies within an organization or as a cooperative effort between different organizations. A participatory future study needs a project and process leader with high competence in methods as well as a broad, general future competence who works with with participants from the organization(s) and eventually external experts.

The work is carried out as a series of seminars in which the group goes through all phases from tracking and analysing to generating alternatives. Between the seminars the members take on different tasks, external studies are conducted and various activities undertaken.

The primary strength of this kind of method is that the organization will own the result.

TIMELINE-BASED METHODS

Archetypal development patterns

The dominant archetypal development patterns are:

- win–lose
- challenge–response
- evolution.

Aside from these three there are a number of other basic patterns that can be observed. In practice the development within an area can be described with a combination of some of the archetypal development patterns below.

- *Winners and losers,* or zero-sum game. The basic concept that drives this scenario is that the world is limited and that life is a zero-sum game. Conflicts are obvious in these kinds of scenarios. Winner–loser is the given basis of every soap opera. A variant of this pattern is 'Save what can be saved' – a not too unusual scenario.
- *Challenge and response,* or the law of pressure and counter-pressure. This is the scenario of obstinate hope. Humanity tends to manage the challenges that are encountered. Living systems like companies and organizations have an amazingly strong ability to adapt and manage challenges. One example of this scenario was Japan's response to the oil price shock in 1973, which led to a total restructuring of its industry.
- *The show goes on,* evolution, or biological development. Evolution means continuous change in one direction, downwards or upwards. At first the development is slow; after some time it accelerates and finally it starts to decline. This is a dominant pattern that also can be used to predict future development. Introduction of new technology is a typical example of evolution.
- *Revolution,* or the big leap. Revolutions are a kind of discontinuity; the development takes a totally new track. Examples of discontinuities are volcanic eruptions, meltdowns and other occurrences that radically change the situation within an area. The microprocessor is an example of such an occurrence that has totally changed the life of organizations. Revolutions very often lead to paradigm shifts and new perspectives on the world.
- *What goes around comes around,* or cyclic patterns. Cyclic patterns are common within the economy. Trade fluctuations and Kondratieff waves are two examples. Cyclic patterns are often treacherous. When there is a boom it is easy to think that everything is good. Very often companies and countries tend to think they themselves have created the success.
- *Through death to life,* or the Phoenix scenario. Through death to life is a scenario of total break up, reconsideration and

rebirth. Or a matter of getting back against all odds. It is, however, more common in fiction than in the real world.

- *Palmy days,* or infinite possibilities. This is perhaps the most common notion of development. Infinite possibilities are the basis for investments and desire to buy. The late 1980s and the 'new economy' boom around the turn of the millennium shift are two obvious examples of how investors as well as consumers saw infinite possibilities.

Trend extrapolation through time-series analysis

Statistical analysis of time series is a method of generating forecasts based on historic data. The method is regularly used within the economic sphere. With the help of simple spreadsheets like Microsoft Excel it is possible to do relatively powerful analyses.

The method can be used to follow the development of one variable, for example the development of travel within a country. If you register data over a period you can apply different regression models to the data to search for the model that fits the data best. The forecast will then be based on the model. The result is presented as graphs, numeric values and margins of error.

Multivariate analysis and multivariate time series analysis

If the number of variables that interrelate is large and the causal links are ambiguous it is sometimes still possible to find patterns with the help of methods for multivariate analysis, such as factor analysis, multiple regression, multi-dimensional scaling and so on. It is however a prerequisite that the area is only apparently and not genuinely complex. A genuinely complex system is unpredictable. It can develop in any direction and it is impossible to foresee the development with better precision than purely random values. In a system that is only apparently complex there are some basic patterns, even if vague, that are possible to identify. The development of the system is predictable, at least in the short term.

Analogies

It is often fruitful to work with historical analogies. The question you ask is 'Is there something else that resembles this?' Analogies are everywhere. Leadership in organizations has lately been compared to conducting an orchestra or playing bass in a jam session. Companies are described as animals or fruits. The multicultural society has been compared to a big fruit salad. Cars are animals – Jaguar. Leadership tests present personalities as animals.

Historical analogies are also popular. The revolution of the late 1990s was described as a new Industrial Revolution, or alternatively it is said that we are entering a new era of hunters or nomads where small independent groups operate on their own or in occasional constellations. One can describe the tool Genghis Khan used to run his empire as the ability to coordinate small mobile bands of robbers.

The value of thinking in analogies is that they open new perspectives, widen the horizon and stimulate creativity.

Here are a few examples of analogical questions:

- If our industry were an ecosystem – which one would it be?
- If our field of industry were a car – which car, who would be at the wheel?
- If our time were another epoch – which epoch?

Long wave

Many societal changes seem to follow long-wave patterns. These are generated by a dialectical interplay between forces and counterforces and also by leaps in technology and social systems. As long ago as 1926 the Russian political economist Kondratieff discovered a pattern of long economic waves from the birth of industrialization to the 1920s.[23] Interest in long economic waves became popular once again during the repercussions of the oil crisis and the economic stagnation of the 1970s.

A long economic wave is supposed to extend for 50 to 60 years and is initiated by one or several technological breakthroughs that affect all areas of society. These innovations are followed by investments in infrastructure, and by new organizational patterns, social contracts and life styles. The long waves of the past century have been impelled by electromechanical innovations (1880–1930) and the car and oil industries (1930–1980).

In the periods preceding a new wave, society is affected by depression, speculation and political turmoil. Whether the early 2000s is such an in-between period, or whether we are heading for a new upturn is a subject of debate.

S-curve analysis

It is a well-known fact that many changes in society follow biologi-cal patterns of growth and decay. By applying theories of biological growth patterns it is possible to make good future predictions, in the same way that we can predict the growth of a child during the first five years. The reason for this is that the growth of children, with very little variation, follows an S-curve. At first the growth rate is low. Then it takes off, and finally slows down again as the child reaches adulthood.

It is not only children who follow this S-curve. The entrance of innovations on a market follows the same pattern. Thus it was possible in 1905, when only 1 per cent of US households had a car, to predict that around 50 per cent of households would have a car sometime between 1920 and 1925! How? Through extrapolating the growth curve from the years up to 1905.

Paradigm shifts[24]

It is often difficult to judge whether a new question or a phenomenon is something that is entirely new – in other words, whether it is a new trend, a new paradigm – or if it is only ephemeral, a fad that will vanish as quick as it came. The word paradigm comes from the Greek and means model or a pattern of a curve.

A paradigm is defined as a set of rules and norms (written or unwritten) with two characteristics: first, they establish or define boundaries, and second, they describe how to act within the boundaries in order to obtain success. A paradigm, in other words, is a way for the brain to organize existence. If a paradigm is to be appropriate it has to have an ability to handle the problems that occur.

Every paradigm has a life cycle and a lifespan that is coherent with the changes in the society that surrounds it. New paradigms originate as answers to new situations. Problems pile up and people cannot solve them within the frameworks of the old mental models, the old paradigms. There must be something new. One example of a paradigm shift is the way we view organizations. Until about 1900 the kind of hierarchic organizations that would be so significant for the twentieth century hardly existed. But increasing railway traffic, demands for insurance solutions and a host of other developments created a need for overview and coordination that could not be met by the small and flat organizations of earlier days. During the 1980s and 1990s we have once more changed paradigm as a result of the inability of hierarchical organizations to respond to a rapidly changing environment.

Briefly, you can say that when too many unsolved problems have piled up (see the 'shelf' in the upper left part of Figure A.1), interest in new thinking increases. New ways of looking at things seem to offer possibilities for solving one or several important problems that could not be solved within the framework of the old paradigm. Those who initiated a revised concept of organizations in the last decades of the twentieth century thought that it would solve the problems caused by lack of flexibility and service as well as by increased costs. The catalyst was the need to tackle unsolved problems.

If you want to foresee a paradigm shift you are advised to keep your eyes on the shelf shown in Figure A.1. A new pattern that seems to solve many of the problems on the shelf has a good chance of becoming the new paradigm within the relevant area.

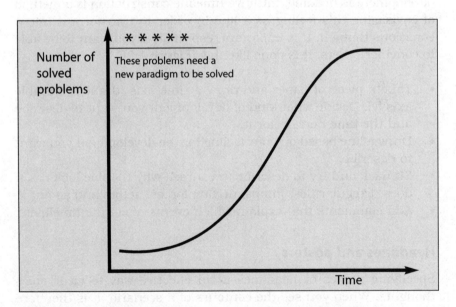

Figure A.1. The paradigm shift and the problems on the shelf
When the number of solved problems levels out, the problems land on the shelf.
Source: Barker, *Future Edge* (1992).

INTUITIVE, GENERATIVE METHODS

Brainstorming

Brainstorming is a well-known method of pushing past blockages of the conscious mind. The principle is to bombard the mind's censors with so much information that they cannot deal with it.

Two things are important. The first is to work under pressure against the clock; a brainstorming session should last no longer than 10 to 15 minutes. The second is to focus on quantitative goals. The aim is to produce as many thoughts as possible in the time; the quality is judged later.

When working on scenarios, brainstorming is an important tool to generate ideas and thoughts. You could for example ask: 'What may affect developments in our arena in the following five to ten years?' or 'What may be the consequences of . . .?'

Intuitive timeline construction

We have spoken about timelines and their possibilities. We have also talked about the way people have an intuitive feeling of where a development is heading. Intuitive timeline construction is a method of envisaging this feeling as a line in order to transform it into a conscious thought. It is important, especially if you want to be able to convince others. It is done like this (Figure A.2):

- Take a piece of paper and draw a time axis (t) and a variable axis (y). Decide what kind of development you want to describe and the time horizon for it.
- Draw a line based on your feeling for the development you want to describe.
- Sit back and try to describe to yourself why the line looks as it does, irregularities, jumps, driving forces, actors and so on.
- Add comments that explain which events affect the timeline.

Headlines and posters

Specifying names or headlines is an effective way to clear one's thoughts. When you see the contours of a scenario, it is therefore important to give them descriptive names. This will help the scenario become clearer to you and it becomes simpler to continue the work and to take the next step.

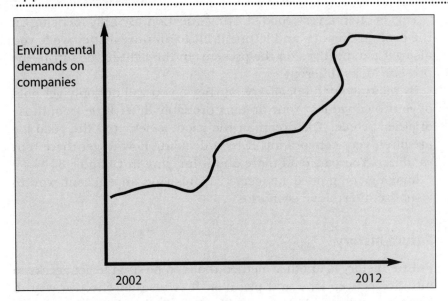

Figure A.2. Example of an intuitive timeline
The constructor thought that by 2004 there would be new restrictions on pollution, and that by 2009 gasoline would not be permitted as car fuel in cities.

The headline describes the essence of the scenario rather than the details. You can work with headlines in the following way:

- Think of the area you work in; if you could make a trip five years into the future, what headlines would you then see that describe this area?
- Formulate a couple of headlines and perhaps a short introduction to the article that would follow them.
- Analyse your headlines and introductions. What could make the development to go this way: driving forces, actors and so on? What will this mean for you?

The headline method is also a good way to train your ability to mould pictures of the future. It can be accompanied by writing articles, which is an effective way to write scenarios.

Imaging

If you had a chance to travel five years into the future and visit your company, what would you then like to see?

This is often a very good starting question. By fully focusing on the desired dream – and letting it lift to an unrealistic level – you also get perspectives on the present. In the light of the future the present looks different.

By making such imaginary journeys, you will not only get hold of your own values. Your dreams probably differ little from those of other people. The dream of the good society and the good life are often very concordant. It is in deciding how to get there that we differ. You can read more about imaging in Chapter 3.

Imaging, or guided imagery, can also be an efficient way to visualize alternative scenarios.

Future history

Future history is another method that can be used to get access to intuitive conceptions and pictures. It is also an effective way to bring scenarios and visions to life. By telling a future history we provide ourselves with 'memories from the future'; in other words, we create memory tracks in the cerebral cortex.

To be able to write a future history – that is, a retrospective scenario – we need a future situation to start from. But this can be intuitive and need not be very clear to us. It is done like this:

- Decide upon the area you want to describe
- Turn on a tape recorder, pick up a pencil and a paper or sit down by the computer. Let the creativity flow. Some incomplete sentences that can start the flow of the creativity can be 'A lot has happened during the last seven years' or 'Nothing is the same anymore'.
- An alternative is to interview yourself. Imagine that someone makes an interview with you in five or ten years time and puts a lot of tricky questions. Answer them!
- Analyse your future history. What was the course of events, breakthroughs, actors and the like? Are there any useful ideas that you can utilize in strategic work? Other lessons?

Paradoxes

Many authors have observed that this is a time of paradoxes. Amongst these Charles Handy and John Naisbitt are probably the most well known.[25] Look at the following examples and you will understand why it is important to take a look at paradoxes.

- *The knowledge paradox:* Knowledge is the new raw material of the new capital and therefore the owners want to lock it in. But on one hand knowledge that is locked away has no value, and on the other hand it is not easily locked up.
- *The organizational paradox:* We find our security in organizations, but if the organizations are to be able to support security they have to become more effective, flexible and insecure.
- *The generation paradox:* Every generation sees itself as different from its predecessors, but expects coming generations to be the same as it is.
- *The information paradox:* The more information we encounter, the more important it is to sort out that information.
- *The size paradox:* Multinational companies become bigger and more influential, but are at the same time divided into smaller and more independent units.

ACTOR-ORIENTED METHODS

Actor analysis/competitor analysis

With a dramaturgic perspective on the future it is easy to realize the role of the actors. The performances and motives of old and new actors develop the story on the stage.

The problem of analysing the future behaviour of the actors on tomorrow's stage is that it is difficult to immerse oneself in their motives and hidden strategies. It is also difficult to foresee new actors on the market. The method has, however, many advantages. The foremost is perhaps that an actor analysis helps us to see different paths to the future, and the future looks less predetermined than it does if we only look at trends in the environment.

An actor analysis is conducted the following way (see Figure A.3):

- Make a list of all actors that in any way can have an influence on the area you are looking at. A mind-map is a helpful tool.

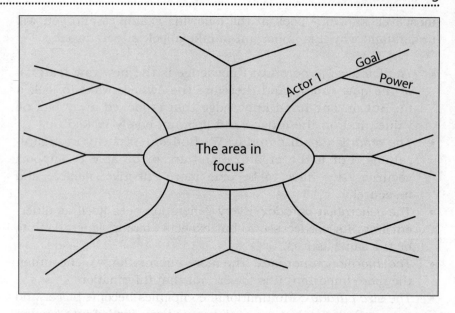

Figure A.3. Model for an actor analysis using the mind-mapping technique

- Identify the motives, goals and power of every actor. If the actor consists of many players with separate interests, or if there are subgroups with separate interests, break up the actor into more groups. What are their strategies? What could make them change strategy?
- Are there any alliances between different actors? What kind of alliances could emerge if you look at goals and interests?
- Are there any new actors that could come up and take a role in the play? What could make them do it?
- How strong are the different actors? What power and influence do they have?
- Considering each actor's goals, where do you believe they are heading?
- What kind of scenarios can you see emerging from this actor-oriented reasoning?

Competitor watch

Competitor watch is a model for continuous monitoring of the actors in the arena that are competitors today or who may become competitors, even if today they are acting in another line of industry. It is often important to look for the latter group. Very often new competition comes from actors nobody has seen as potential competitors before. The banks in Sweden were very aware that they would face tougher competition from niche banks and insurance companies, but they were taken completely by surprise when the two biggest retail chains started banks.

When these kinds of opportunities are identified it is important to put them on the competitor watch list.

Value-chain analysis

Industry-level value-chain analysis is an effective way to reveal the interplay between different players in a specific industry. Value-chain analysis describes the activities within and around an organization and relates them to an analysis of the organization's competitive strength. It was originally introduced as a counting analysis to shed light on the 'value added' by separate steps in a complex manufacturing process. In the early 1980s Michael Porter linked that analysis to competitive analysis and the modern form of value-chain thinking was born.

Value-chain analysis is often a good starting point in a scenario-planning project. Through the analysis you get a good understanding of the present strengths and weaknesses of the existing industry. The more complex the business ecosystem is, the more complex the value chains become. Often there are several intersecting value chains, as has been common for instance in the telecom and media industries. Value-chain analysis is a powerful tool: a good understanding of the value chain helps in the construction of solid scenarios.

CONSEQUENCE-FOCUSED METHODS
Issues management

Issues management is a kind of combination of trend watch and actor analysis. The task of the issues manager is to record and handle questions related to public opinion, social trends, new technology and so on that may have an impact on the organization. In a way, that person tracks changes in the surrounding world, but at the same time the task is often also to deal with such questions and suggest ways to affect their development. It is important to emphasize that issues are not only problems but rather positive or negative questions whose importance may increase and affect the business in the long run.

In that sense, issues management could be considered an organizational process related to foresight.[26] The task is:

1. To identify, monitor and analyse social, technological, political and economical driving forces and trends that can affect a trade or an organization.
2. Interpret and define consequences and choices. The earlier a new question can be identified and understood, the greater one's freedom of action will be.
3. Start short and long-term activities in order to deal with the situation that has arisen. The earlier the organization acts, the greater chance it has to formulate strategies that support the long-term goals.

Questions move from the unknown periphery into the centre of public life. Sometimes this happens very fast; sometimes it takes a long time. However, a couple of conditions need to be met for a question to take off from being hidden and unknown and establish a place on the public agenda. It requires:

• A context: a mental and social preparedness.
• A key event: something that thrusts the question upon the general common awareness, a trigger that media can make good use of.
• A name: the name or label that helps to keep it in mind (e.g. Watergate).
• A carrier: a person who pushes the question into the public domain.

These insights could also be used in the promotion of new issues.

Single-impact analysis (SIM)

There are a number of methods for the systematic evaluation of impacts of possible events. The effects of implementing new technology (technology assessment) and the impact of environmental changes (environmental impact analysis) are two examples of such changes. We call these kinds of analysis single-impact analyses, as they deal with a one-directional impact.

When you conduct a single-impact analysis it is necessary to have something to start with, for example a step or a list of steps, a scenario or some alternative scenarios. This means that impact analysis can be used within a wide range of areas – for example to evaluate the impacts of different scenarios on a field of industry, or different strategies abilities that may help deal with different scenarios or trends. The WUS analysis that is described in Chapter 3 of this book is an example of a single-impact analysis where strategies are assessed towards three different dimensions. (See Figure A.4.)

Consequence tree

Very often it takes some time before the really big effects of a new technology or an occurrence are felt, and the effects are very often indirect. If you do an impact analysis it is therefore often important to get a good grip on the consequences in the long run and the second, third and fourth-rank consequences. By working with consequence chains and consequence trees it is often possible to identify these. A consequence tree is a less systematic and more creative method than the single-impact analysis that is described above.

In Chapter 3 (section on Deciding) we gave a more detailed description of how consequence trees can be used in future analysis and idea generation.

Future event production

Future event production is a creative method to produce large amounts of future events intuitively or more systematically. This

Step/Alternative	Scenario 1	Scenario 2	Scenario 3	Scenario 4
1. Xxxx	++	+	– –	–
2. Yyyy	–	+/–	+	++
3. Vvvv	++	++	+	+
4. Zzzz	–	++	–	– –

Figure A.4. Single-impact analysis
An example where certain strategic steps/alternatives have been assessed according to how well they work in four different scenarios.

can be done through simple brainstorming where each event is written down on a sticky note, or through a more systematic consequence analysis where the consequences function as fuel for the creative process.

After the events have been generated they can be clustered and structured in time. Contradictory predictions are resolved and a plausible timeline (or several timelines) are constructed. During that process new events are added.

Future event production is an effective way to put flesh and blood on base scenarios or alternative scenarios. It is a method commonly used by film producers and writers.

Probability effects

This is a method for a quick evaluation of the impact of a trend, change, or phenomenon that makes it easier to concentrate on essentials. It is based on the fact that there are two aspects of every change or phenomenon: the probability that it will happen, and the consequences if it happens. The process is simple:

- List all your changes or trends.
- Assess the probability of each and every one happening on a scale 0–100 (or just as low, medium, high). If it is a trend, try to judge its strength.
- Assess the consequences on a scale 0–100 (or just low, medium, high). It can often be helpful to separate long and short-term consequences.
- Set out the changes as in Figure A.5.
- Focus on probable changes with extensive consequences.

Through combining this kind of analysis with judgement of your present knowledge of each trend or phenomenon it is possible to gain a picture of the knowledge gaps.

Check every trend or occurrence and note down your knowledge about the question (see Figure A.6). You need to consider both the quantity and the authenticity of your information. In this way it is possible to frame the issues that should be in focus for collecting information and analysis. Mark them with a ring in the diagram. If the questions are within the critical area in Figure A.5, it is extremely important to improve the authenticity by seeking more information.

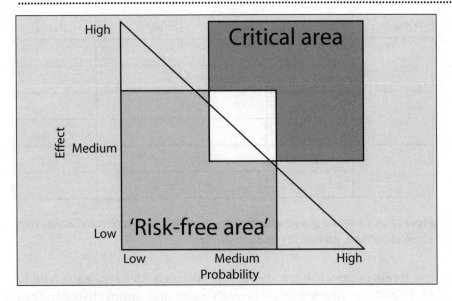

Figure A.5. Probability effects
Energy should be concentrated on the upper right corner, the darkly shaded area. In the upper left part are the wild cards, changes that are unlikely but would have major effects.

SYSTEMS METHODS

Complexity and uncertainty analysis

Mapping the complexity and speed of the business environment is often a good starting point. Increased complexity means increased opportunities, but also unforeseeable threats. Some changes in the business environment are linear, some are not. Figure A.7 sets out a few questions that could indicate the degree of raplexity in the business environment. The first six questions are related to complexity and complex, unpredictable change. Numbers 7–12 are more related to change in general, not indicating complexity.

In the raplexity diagram (Figure A.8) you can plot each business unit and product area, or the entire company environment. The appropriateness of scenario planning differs from ecosystem to ecosystem. As seen in Figure A.9, at lower levels of uncertainty (and discrete uncertainties) other scenario methods should be used than when there is a large extent of continuous uncertainty. The appropriate strategies also differ between ecosystems. At very

Trend	Time-horizon	Probability	Effect	Knowledge
1.	Short			
	Long			
2.	Short			
	Long			
3.	Short			
	Long			

Figure A.6. Example of a scheme that can be helpful for a collected assessment of trends, effects, probability and knowledge

low levels of uncertainty an appropriate proactive strategy could be to introduce uncertainty through new and innovative strategic moves. At higher levels of uncertainty, creating stability and certainty in the market is usually the most effective way to get a leading position (at least for dominating players).

Cross-impact analysis (CIM)

Cross-impact analysis is a method that helps us to see how different trends or actions affect each other or to analyse the interrelationships between variables within a system. The method is sometimes called structure analysis. It can be used to identify the interplay between variables, trends, actions and so forth. It can be seen as a kind of extended consequence analysis. The information it adds is a picture of the interplay between the trends and variables and, not least important, a picture of what is dependent, what is independent, what is driving and what is driven by others. A cross-impact analysis is very helpful when you want to make sure of identifying key variables and trends.

A cross-impact analysis can be carried out in a simple and informal way by a small team in the following way:

1. The prerequisite is a list of trends or key variables to analyse. It is often best to identify the variables as trends with a certain direction.
2. Create a scheme (see Figure A.10) and fill in your variables.

	Completely disagree						Completely agree
1. Actions taken by my firm will affect our competitors strongly	1	2	3	4	5	6	7
2. Our business environment is very complex with many unclear factors and relationships influencing our firm	1	2	3	4	5	6	7
3. It is very difficult to foresee change	1	2	3	4	5	6	7
4. New and unpredictable competition is constantly occurring	1	2	3	4	5	6	7
5. There are many unforeseen threats that we have to cope with	1	2	3	4	5	6	7
6. The performance of our firm is highly influenced by unpredictable public policies	1	2	3	4	5	6	7
7. The market will grow for several years	1	2	3	4	5	6	7
8. The business opportunities for the next 12 months look good	1	2	3	4	5	6	7
9. Our customers' preferences are continually changing	1	2	3	4	5	6	7
10. Social values in society are continually changing	1	2	3	4	5	6	7
11. The business environment is continually changing	1	2	3	4	5	6	7
12. The innovation rate in the market is high	1	2	3	4	5	6	7
Complexity (questions 1–6):							
Change (questions 7–12):							

Figure A.7. Example of complexity and uncertainty analysis

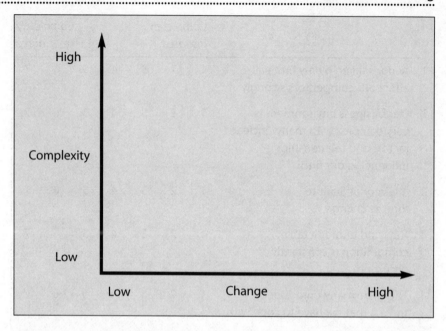

Figure A.8. Raplexity diagram to plot a business ecosystem's raplexity (complexity and speed of change)

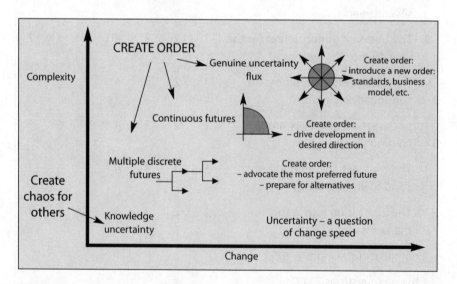

Figure A.9. Different types of uncertainties on different complexity levels and their matching strategies[27]

Trend/Variable	1	2	3	4	5	6	Sum
1		-2	-1	2	0	1	6
2	2		0	0	0	0	2
3	-1	0		0	2	0	3
4	-2	2	1		2	1	8
5	2	0	2	0		-1	5
6	0	2	-2	2	-1		7
Sum	7	6	6	4	5	3	

Strongest
driver

↑
**Strongest
dependent**

Figure A.10. Example of cross-impact analysis with six trends or variables
Variable Number 4 is the strongest driver and Number 1 most dependent
(driven by others). The result is summarized in absolute terms.

3. Go through the scheme systematically and judge square by
   square the extent to which trend A will influence trend B: positively, negatively or not at all. Mark it with a number on the
   scale –2 to + 2.
4. It is now possible to summarize the result. The sum of each
   row indicates how strongly driving the variable is; that is, to
   what extent it influences other variables. The sum of each
   column indicates the level of dependence of each variable.
   Now it is also possible to plot the trends in a diagram, with
   dependence on one axis and driving on the other.

When the trends/variables are plotted into a diagram, as in Figure
A.11, the patterns become even clearer.

   The strength of this simple kind of cross-impact analysis is that it
helps you to clarify your presumptions and detect incoherent ideas.
When you work in a group, it also leads to fruitful discussions.
Another very important point is that you get a clear picture of which
trends are drivers and which are dependent. By analysing the interplay between different variables it is also possible to identify certain

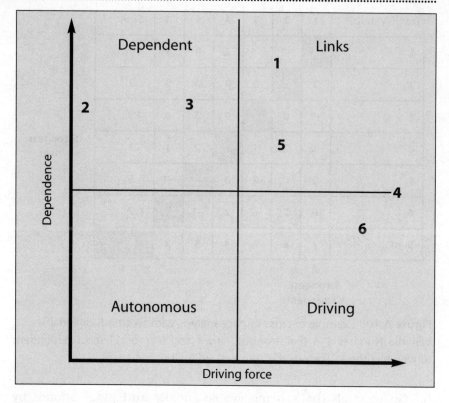

Figure A.11. Cross-impact diagram

parts of the system. In Chapter 3, in the section on Tracking, there is a description of how a cross-impact analysis can be used as a basis for a causal-loop diagram that shows the interplay between the trends.

A cross-impact analysis is a very useful tool when it comes to qualitative analysis of complex problems.

Four-field analysis

Four-field analysis is a simple way to generate simple scenarios by using key variables from, for example, a cross-impact analysis. The key variables may be continuous variables, describing a long series of conditions on continuous scale, for example the number of 3G users in a country. They can also be more discrete: occurrences that may or may not happen. (You can find two examples of four-field scenario constructions in the section on Analysing in Chapter 3.)

Systems analysis

Systems analysis has lately become a popular tool to describe and analyse complex systems. Systems theory is frequently used within automatic-control engineering, which deals with regulating simple or more complex systems through different forms of feedback loops. But systems theory is also the basis of, for example, modern family therapy.

Systems analysis is built upon two basic assumptions. The first is that the parts of a system can only be understood in context, by taking the totality into consideration. Second, in order to understand the whole, it is necessary to identify the parts and their internal interplay.

The strengths of systems theory are, first, that it makes it possible to handle big, complex, 'real' systems and, second, that it is possible to create working models of the reality.

There are basically two different types of systems: those with positive feedback and those with negative feedback. The first kind of system is self-reinforcing. An increase in one part of the system strengthens other parts and vice versa. These systems must be strictly controlled from the outside if they are not to drive themselves to destruction.

Examples of escalating systems are found in many places in the real world: money, power, success, knowledge and population follow its rules. A typical example is mice in a closed room. If there are no other restrictions, such as lack of food, they will very quickly fill the room as they breed at a furious rate. Another example is car traffic

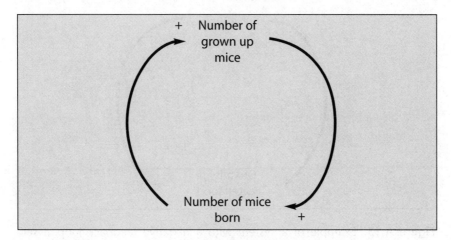

Figure A.12. Example of a positive feedback loop, self-reinforcing system

and roads. Wider and better roads relieve traffic jams for a transitional period, but the attentive motorist will have noticed that more people bring out their cars when the queues have diminished. When we talk of virtuous and vicious circles in organizations we are usually talking about positive feedback systems.

Negative feedback systems are active and self-regulating. They have an internal drive towards balance and use energy continuously. An increase in one part of the system leads to decrease in another part. One example of a negative feedback system is the sense of balance itself; another is supply and demand. The cycle of hunger and eating is another very commonly experienced balanced system. When we are hungry we eat more, and the more we eat, the less hungry we will be.

The examples of hunger and traffic jams also illustrate another eccentricity in systems: delay. 'Now I have eaten too much,' is a common comment from someone who had felt very hungry when sitting down at the table. The feeling of satisfaction does not come immediately: it is delayed. The same goes with traffic jams and new roads. It takes time to digest one's food or realize that the roads are less congested, which means that it takes some time before people discover the new situation.

The consequence is that systems have a tendency to swing. Everyone who has tried to regulate the hot water in a shower with two taps knows what it is all about. At first the water is too cold

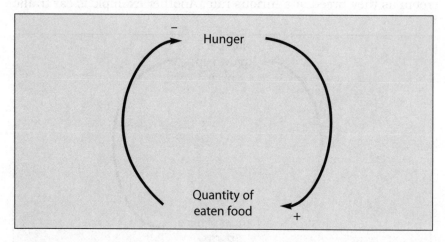

Figure A.13. Example of a system with a negative feedback loop, a self-regulating system

because the pipes are long. We turn the hot water tap full on and all of the sudden the water is boiling hot. We quickly turn down the hot water and turn up the cold, and now it is too cold. We throttle down the cold water again and so on until we have achieved the temperature we want.

The characteristic of a self-regulating system is that it swings towards a state of equilibrium. A system with insufficient dampening can get into an accelerating self-swing that leads to greater and greater swings and finally to the breakdown of the system. This is hardly the case in our example of the shower.

Causal mapping/causal-loop diagrams

Using the reasoning above it is possible to describe your system as a set of feedback loops. Such clusters of subsystems linked with feedback loops are usually called causal-loop diagrams. Describing a system in a causal-loop diagram is an effective way to achieve clarity about systemic interplay and system dynamics. By drawing a loop diagram it is possible to realize weaknesses of a system, to identify key factors, alternative scenarios and so on.

In Figure A.14 we have described a common situation in a small company. More work means more money and increasing resources for marketing. But correspondingly, there is a lack of time for

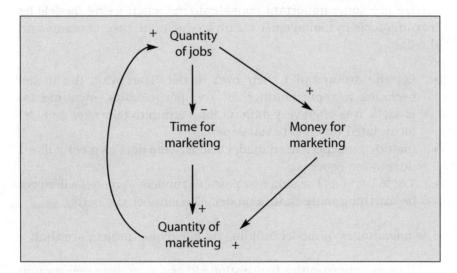

Figure A.14. Illustration of a common situation for small companies

marketing activities, and this hampers the marketing efforts that are a prerequisite for more jobs in the long run.

There are some rules to keep in mind when you work with causal-loop diagrams. These are:

- Try to give quantitative descriptions to all variables (number of jobs, cost, time, etc.).
- Identify all variables positively (not necessary, but it facilitates the thinking).
- If links between variables need to be explained, add an explaining interlink.
- Close all loops.

As we have mentioned the result of a cross-impact analysis can easily be interpreted into a causal-loop diagram (see Chapter 3, sections on Analysing and Deciding).

System analysis as a tool for learning

Working with systems in this way has become increasingly popular. One very important application is learning. What happens when you develop a model of your system is that you make your own mental models clear to yourself. You get your own presumptions around the interplay down on paper.

Here are some important considerations when using models as learning tools in management teams, education, project teams and the like:

- Let the group build their own model. That way, the model becomes a representation of the participants' own mental models. It is often very difficult for a group to take over a model formulated by an external expert.
- Include an experienced model builder who acts as a consultant during the process.
- Try to build as the simplest possible models. A model will never be anything more than a model. The simpler the better.

The advantages of model building as a learning project are that:

- It gives opportunities to question old and introduce new mental models.

- It creates learning.
- It creates understanding of the interplay within the system; our intuitive understanding of complex interplay very often fits badly to reality.
- It enables us to make risk-free experiments in an artificial environment, a micro-world.
- It forces the participants to express thoughts explicitly and logically.
- It reveals interplay and complexity.

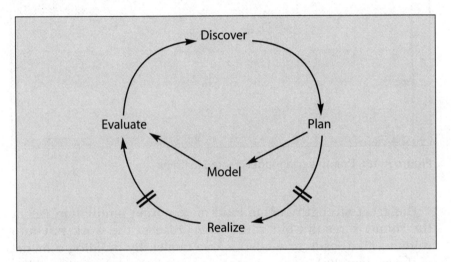

Figure A.15. Advantages of system models

With the help of system models we can shorten the time needed for learning and running new systems. Once we have discovered new connections and got ourselves a mental model, we can test it in a created microworld that models the real world.

Systems modelling/dynamic simulation[28]

With the help of simple simulation programs it is possible to make models for complex dynamic systems. Stella™ and Ithink™ from High Performance Systems[29] are among the most widespread programs. The first requirement is to describe your system, using the special system language that makes it possible to make mathematics out of the connections.

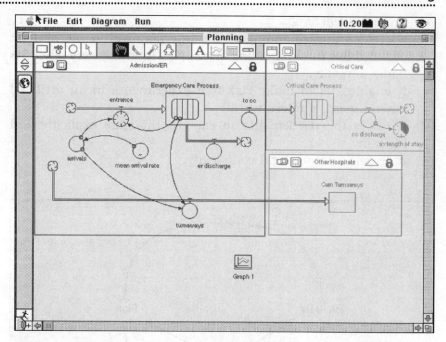

Figure A.16. Example of a model created in Ithink

The great strength of this kind of computer simulation is not the numeric results but rather the process, the work put into thinking that leads to a sustainable model. By building a model of the system, linking the parts into the whole and specifying the connections, you can obtain an understanding of the system that cannot be achieved in any other way. By experimenting with different kinds of connections and similar aspects you get an understanding of the sensitivity of the system.

This kind of mathematical model building also plays a popular role in the kind of leader training that we have mentioned above.

Appendix 2: Glossary

Actor

An actor is an individual, group, organization or even a nation that has an interest in the issue or system studied.

Addressee

The addressee is the receiver of the scenario analysis or the proposals based on the analysis. It is important to clarify who the addressees are so as to be able to format the presentation of the results in a desirable format. Quite often, the futures-occupied analyst finds qualified systems modelling interesting, but the decisions-oriented addressee wants a ten-line proposal.

Back-casting

Back-casting is a scenario technique where you start with an imagined future and then create a path to it. The path could be constructed through analytical methods or through more creative methods such as future history writing.

Base scenario

A base scenario gives a broad picture of what we can take for granted in the future. It summarizes general assumptions about the future on which a number of contrasted alternative scenarios can be built. Thus, a base scenario is a very broadly and qualitatively described forecast where built-in uncertainties are hidden. Those uncertainties can, however, be highlighted in alternative scenarios.

The base scenario gives indications of the essential actions that organizations need to take in order to be able to cope with the future.

Business intelligence

Business intelligence is the term for the collection and analysis of business critical information. Business intelligence could be divided into market intelligence, competitor intelligence, technology intelligence and similar elements relating to the purpose of the activity.

Conflicts   Conflicts can occur as a result of actors' conflicting interests. They are often a strong driver in social change. Potential conflicts could be used as an inspirational source in scenario development. It is also important to consider important conflict dimensions in each scenario of a scenario set.

Contextual analysis   Contextual analysis is a term for all sorts of analysis of the organization's external environment, the outside world.

Dystopian scenario   A dystopian scenario is a real nightmare scenario. Dystopian scenarios are common in literature, Orwell's *1984* is one example of dystopia in metaphorical format. Dystopian scenarios full of conflicts, such as soap operas, are often exciting and stimulating and are often used as contrasting scenarios to normative and more utopian ones.

Emerging issues   Emerging or potential issues are ones that have not yet come to the fore, but have the potential to become problems that the company will need to act on. Potential future issues are often identified through scenario processes.

EPISTLE   The Apostle Paul wrote the Epistle to the Romans. Here the word helps us to remember six areas that are often important to check when you trace changes in the surrounding world.
- Economy and market
- Politics
- Institutions and organizations
- Social changes
- Technology
- Legal changes
- Ecology and ethics.

Event   A future event is something that may or may not happen in the future. Scenarios can be created by generating and clustering future events.

Forecast or prognosis   A forecast is a description of the most probable future under present conditions. Forecasts are useful in the short term, but rapidly lose their significance in the longer term as they do not take future events into

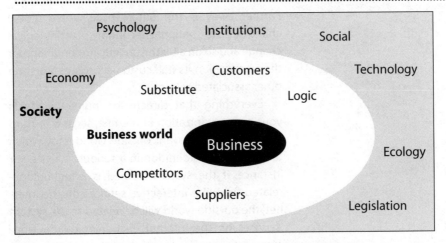

Figure A. 17. EPISTLE: a system for scanning the environment

account. Assessments of economic conditions are common examples of forecasts.

Foresight

While 'forecast' is used as a term for predictions, foresight is a term that describes a more open perspective on futuristic thinking. Foresights focus on the identification of possible futures, potential issues, tendencies, and uncertainties, often using scenario methods. Foresight is similar to the term prospective analysis (see below).

Futures study

All types of studies concerned with the exploration and analysis of future states beyond normal budget horizons could be named futures studies. Traditionally, the term applies to studies with a 10–30-year horizon.

Normative scenario

A normative scenario is one that describes a desired (or undesirable) future. The purpose of normative scenarios is sometimes to explore the best-case future and possible roads to that future. The purpose could also be communicative.

Outside world/ business environment

For an organization, the outside world is everything that exists outside it. The closest part of this world is the industry and the market, where customers, competitors, owners, financers, authorities and suppliers are active. The actions of these players affect the underlying conditions for the organization.

Further away is the outer space where global changes, the national economy, technological change and so on alter the underlying conditions for the organization, its staff, customers, competitors and other associated actors.

Everything that directly or indirectly affects your own organization in the first, second or third stage is thus a relevant outside-world issue worth taking into consideration in a serious analysis. For instance, if the system studied is a technology-related field like 'interactive services on the Internet', the outside world will be related to the system 'services on the Internet'. Technological development, rate of growth and the like then belong to the outside world.

By definition, the outside world is the future because what is happening in it will reach us after a certain amount of delay. We know, for example, that as a rule what is happening in the United States reaches Europe within a few months or years.

An analysis of the outside world is usually a first step in a scenario planning process that begins with the question: What is happening and what might happen in the outside world that is of significance to us in the long term?

Pitfalls

A pitfall is a trap you could fall into. There are many pitfalls in scenario work. There are prejudices, wishful thinking and blind spots that could lead to lousy analysis. And several other traps lurk in the fields of process design, selection of participants, communication format and the others.

Prospective

This term is used by Michel Godet and others to designate a multiplicity of possible futures. Like many others, Godet is critical of the possibility of making forecasts and probability-based assessments of the future. Prospective analysis generates scenarios based on a series of suppositions about the right path to choose.

Qualitative scenario methods

Qualitative methods are based on soft data (that is, non-quantifiable variables) and reasoning. The

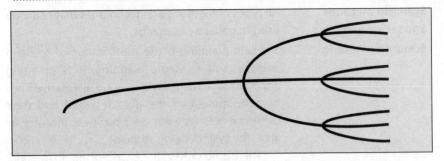

Figure A. 18. The prospective view of the future as a multiplicity of alternatives

purpose is often to identify and analyse systems relations, key actors, uncertainties and the like. Qualitative methods are necessary in medium to long-range planning.

Semi-qualitative methods such as trend-impact and cross-impact analyses are common in scenario planning. By semi-qualitative we mean methods where for instance relations are quantified on the basis of qualitative reasoning.

Quantitative scenario methods

The purpose of quantitative methods is to get output data in numbers. Quantitative methods are based on the assumption of causality that can be captured in regression or systems models. Quantitative scenarios could often be modelled in spreadsheets or desktop simulation programs.

Quantitative methods are often a necessary complement to qualitative methods in the search for more solid facts and figures, and in the exploration of the future trajectories of present trends and patterns.

Scenario

A scenario is the full description of a future state and the path to that future. A complete scenario should, over the time period the scenario covers, give answers to the question: 'Who does what, when, where and for what reason?' Scenarios are often presented as snapshots of the future.

Scenario learning

Scenario learning is the use of scenario techniques to increase shared understandings of systems dynamics, future developments, uncertainties and so on. Scenario learning is by nature explorative.

Scenario methods and techniques

All types of methods and techniques that could be used to generate scenarios.

Scenario planning

Scenario planning is the combination of scenario analysis and strategic planning. It is planning aimed at systematically exploring alternative lines of development in the outside world and their consequences for your own business, industry or area (the system being studied).

There is no universal scenario-planning method. Instead, there are a large number of different techniques and methods for generating and using scenarios in planning and decision-making contexts. If anything, scenario planning should be looked on as an attitude, an approach to the future, in combination with a set of methods.

System

A system consists of a set of combined parts or elements. To assess its development it is first necessary to understand its structure. Systems analysis aims at describing and analysing the interplay between the elements so as to be able to draw up a practical working model of the system, e.g. a company and the world about it.

Trends as opposed to fads

Trends are long-term, often irreversible, changes that frequently take place over a number of years and which often creep up imperceptibly. The effect of a strong trend on a phenomenon can often be measured and forecast.

Fads are more short-term shifts, for example in interests and opinion. The difference between trends and fads is similar to that between climate and weather.

Vision

A vision is a vivid picture of a desired future, often expressed in a short and pithy way. If it is to work as a 'strategic vision' in an organization, it must be well anchored in the hearts of those who are to make it come true. Every scenario-planning process should be connected to a vision of what you want to achieve.

Utopian scenario

A utopian scenario is a normative best-case scenario that lacks in plausibility and therefore lies beyond the space of possible, credible futures. Utopian scenarios are often conflict-free and relatively boring. That is also the reason why they are so rare in literature.

Wild card   Unlikely future events that would have great impact if they occurred are usually called wild cards. Wild cards create discontinuities in the development curve. Scenarios can be generated around wild cards, but wild cards are usually sifted out in scenario processes and treated separately.

Notes

1. See for instance the scenarios in *Beyond Mobile* (Lindgren, Jedbratt, Svensson) developed during autumn 2000.
2. Strategy and performance (Miller 1987; Mosalowski 1993; McDougall *et al.* 1994; Dess *et al.* 1997), decision process and performance (Fredrickson and Mitchell 1984; Eisenhardt 1989; Judge and Miller 1991), top management team characteristics and performance (Eisenhardt and Bourgeois 1988; Smith *et al.* 1994; Gelatkanycz and Hambrick 1997), strategy and structure (Miles and Snow 1978; Miller 1987; Lyles and Schwenk 1992; Jennings and Seaman 1994).
3. For an in-depth description, see Mats Lindgren's doctoral thesis *Strategic Flexibility: Antecedents and Performance Implications.* Henley Management College/Brunel University 2001.
4. See for instance Haeckel and Nolan (1993).
5. The response rate was 20 per cent. All variables were measured on multiple-item Likert scales.
6. In conformity with Venkatraman and Ramanujam (1986).
7. See for instance the traditional work of Lawrence and Lorsch (1967) and Thompson (1967).
8. On strategic flexibility see for instance Hopkins and Hopkins (1997).
9. Hitt *et al.* (1998).
10. Which has been strongly advocated by researchers like Nordström and Ridderstråle (1999).
11. See for instance Hamel (1998, 2000) and Johnson and Scholes (1999).
12. For more in-depth descriptions, see for instance Kao (1997) and Krets de Vries (1997).
13. Follow-up studies of Swedish medium-sized and large companies from a wide range of industries have confirmed the results.
14. See Chandler (1962), Ansoff (1965), Lawrence and Lorsch (1967), Thompson (1967) and Andrews 1971.
15. Relevant references on each topic are for instance: strategic decision-making process, Schwenk 1995); hyper-competition and high-velocity environments, D'Aveni (1994) and Brown and Eisenhardt (1997, 1998); organizational capabilities, Barney (1991); and evolutionary aspects of strategy, Brown and Eisenhardt (1997) and Ruef (1997).
16. See for instance Brown and Eisenhardt (1997), Chakravarthy (1997) and Ozsomer *et al.* (1997).

17. See for instance Porter (1996), Brown and Eisenhardt (1997) and Williamson (1999).
18. For a thorough investigation, see for instance Lars-Olof Persson's doctoral thesis *Mood and Expectation*.
19. A phrase that goes back to the early work by Chris Argyris and David Schön in the 1970s.
20. It was introduced by Peter Senge and has been used by, for instance, Peter Schwarz in the context of scenario planning.
21. Rolf Jensen is presently director of Dream Company. The concept of The Call and The Holy Grail will be developed in a forthcoming book.
22. See for instance Shona Brown's and Kathleen Eisenhardt's research on IT-companies presented in *Competing on the Edge* (Brown and Eisenhardt 1998).
23. The conclusions were presented in the book *Long Waves in Economic Life*. His reward was a lifetime vacation in Siberia. The ideas were later picked up by Joseph Schumpeter.
24. Based on the book *Future Edge* (Barker).
25. The books are *The Age of Paradox* (Handy) and *Global Paradox* (Naisbitt).
26. See for instance Joseph Coates' book *Issues Management* (1986).
27. Inspired by Courtney, Kirkland *et al.* (1997). Strategy under uncertainty. *Harvard Business Review* (November–December): 67–79.
28. The pioneer within this area is Jay Forrester who back in 1961 in the book *Industrial Dynamics* formulated the principles for the mathematical modelling of dynamic systems. Forrester was also the man behind the first global resource model that was presented in the book *Limits of Growth* (1972). It is Forester's model for description that is used in Ithink and Stella.
29. http://www.hps-inc.com/

Kairos Future

Kairos Future helps companies establish leading positions in relation to the future, both in theory and in action. We work at all levels in analysing the future and external world, from strategic development to broad change. Our emphasis, however, is on strategic reorientation in the border territory between the future and strategic change.

Our ambition is to combine creative thinking with research that generates new insights and ideas about the future, and to integrate these findings with a practical approach in our consultancy assignments.

Our speciality is carrying out rapid reorientation processes together with our clients, developing long-term sustainable strategies on the basis of scenario analyses.

We also give lectures and organize conferences on the future both on our own behalf and for clients. The Kairos Academy conducts open or internal company training in scenario planning and strategic development, from introductory to university levels. Read more about us at:
www.kairos.se

Contact us at:

Kairos Future
P. O. Box 804
SE-101 36 Stockholm, Sweden
Tel: +46 8 545 225 00
Fax: +46 8 545 225 01
info@kairos.se

References

Andrews, K. (1971). *The Concept of Strategy*. Homewood, IL: Irwin.

Ansoff, H. I. (1965). *Corporate Strategy: An Analytical Approach to Business Policy for Growth and Explanation*. New York: McGraw Hill.

Ashby, W. R. (1956). *An Introduction to Cybernetics*. London: Chapman and Hall.

Barney, J. (1991). 'Firm resources and sustained competitive advantage.' *Journal of Management* 17: 99–120.

Beinhocken, E. D. (1999). 'Robust adaptive strategies.' *Sloan Management Review* 40(3): 95–106.

Bettis, R. A. and M. A. Hitt (1995). 'The new competitive landscape.' *Strategic Management Journal* 16: 7–16.

Blaxill, M. F. and T. M. Hout (1998). 'Make decisions like a fighter pilot.' In: *Perspectives on Strategy*. C. W. Stern and G. J. Stalk. New York: John Wiley.

Boulding, K. E. (1964). *The Meaning of the Twentieth Century*. New York: Prentice-Hall.

Bracker, J. (1980). 'The historical development of strategic management concept.' *Academy of Management Review* 5: 219–24.

Brown, S. L. and K. M. Eisenhardt (1997). 'The art of continuous change: linking complexity theory and time-paced evolution in relentlessly shifting organizations.' *Administrative Science Quarterly* 42: 1–34.

Brown, S. L. and K. M. Eisenhardt (1998). *Competing on the Edge*. Boston, MA: Harvard Business School Press.

Chakravarthy, B. (1997). 'A new strategy framework for coping with turbulence.' *Sloan Management Review* (Winter): 69–82.

Chandler, A. D. (1962). *Strategy and Structure: Chapters in the History of the American Industrial Enterprise*. Cambridge, MA: MIT Press.

Coates, J. F. (1986). *Issues Management. How You Plan, Organize and Manage For The Future*. Bethesda, MD: Lomond.

Collins, J. C. and J. I. Porras (1996). 'Building your company's vision.' *Harvard Business Review* (September–October): 65–77.

D'Aveni, R. (1994). *Hypercompetition: Managing the Dynamics of Strategic Manoeuvering*. New York: Free Press.

Dess, G. G., F. T. Lumpkin and J. G. Covin (1997). 'Entrepreneurial strategy making and firm performance: test of contingency and configurational models.' *Strategic Management Journal* 18(9): 677–95.

Doyle, P. (2000). 'Radical strategies for profitable growth.' *European Management Journal* 16(3): 253–61.

Eisenhardt, K. M. (1989). 'Making fast strategic decisions in high-velocity environments.' *Academy of Management Journal* 33(3): 543–76.

Eisenhardt, K. M. and L. J. Bourgeois III (1988). 'Politics of strategic decision making in high-velocity environments: toward a midrange theory.' *Academy of Management Journal* 31(4): 737–70.

Eisenhardt, K. M. and M. J. Zbaracki (1992). 'Strategic decision making.' *Strategic Management Journal* 13: 17–37.

Feigenbaum, A., S. Hart and D. Schendel (1996). 'Strategic reference point theory.' *Strategic Management Journal* 17: 219–35.

Fredrickson, J. W. and T. R. Mitchell (1984). 'Strategic decision process: comprehensiveness and performance in an industry with an unstable environment.' *Academy of Management Journal* 27(2): 399–423.

Gelatkanycz, M. A. and D. C. Hambrick (1997). 'The external ties of top executives: implications for strategic choice and performance.' *Administrative Science Quarterly* 42: 654–81.

Godet, M. (1987) *Scenarios and Strategic Management*. Butterworths.

Haeckel, S. H. and R. L. Nolan (1993). 'Managing by wire.' *Harvard Business Review* (September–October).

Hamel, G. (1998). 'Strategy innovation and the quest for value.' *Sloan Management Review* (Winter): 7–14.

Hamel, G. (2000). *Leading the Revolution*. Boston, MA: Harvard Business School Press.

Hamel, G. and A. E. Heene (1994). *Competence-Based Competition*. Chichester, UK: John Wiley.

Hamel, G. and C. K. Prahalad (1994). *Competing for the Future*. Boston, MA: Harvard Business School Press.

Hamel, G., C. K. Prahalad, H. Thomas and D. O'Neil, Eds (1998). *Strategic Flexibility*. Strategic management series. Chichester, UK: John Wiley.

Handy, Charles (1995). *The Age of Paradox*. Boston, MA: Harvard Business School Press.

Hart, S. and C. Banbury (1994). 'How strategy-making processes can make a difference.' *Strategic Management Journal* 15: 251–69. (Firms with high process capability outcompete firms with lower capability.)

Hitt, M. A., B. W. Keats and S. A. DeMarie (1998). 'Navigating in the new competitive landscape: building strategic flexibility and competitive advantage in the twenty-first century.' *Academy of Management Executive* 12(4): 22–42.

Hopkins, W. E. and S. A. Hopkins (1997). 'Strategic planning–financial performance relationships in banks: a causal examination.' *Strategic Management Journal* 18: 635–52.

Jennings, D. F. and S. L. Seaman (1994). 'High and low levels of organisational adaptation: an empirical analysis of strategy, structure and performance.' *Strategic Management Journal* 15: 459–75.

Johnson, G. and K. Scholes (1999). *Exploring Corporate Strategy*, 5th edn. London, New York, Singapore: Prentice Hall.

Judge, W. Q. and A. Miller (1991). 'Antecendents and outcomes of decision speed in different environmental contexts.' *Academy of Management Journal* 34(2): 449–63.

Kao, J. (1997). *Jamming: The Art and Discipline of Business*. London: Harper Collins.

Krets de Vries, M. F. R. (1997). 'Creative leadership: jazzing up business.' *Chief Executive* (121): 64–6.

Lawrence, P. R. and J. Lorsch (1967). *Organisation and Environment*. Boston, MA: Harvard University Press.

Lei, D., M. A. Hitt and R. Bettis (1996). 'Dynamic core competences through meta-learning and strategic content.' *Journal of Management* 22(4): 549–69.

Lengnick-Hall, C. A. and J. A. Wolf (1999). 'Similarities and contradictions in the core logic of three strategy research streams.' *Strategic Management Journal* 20: 1109–32.

Lindgren, M., Jedbratt, J. and E. Svensson (2002). *Beyond Mobile*. Basingstoke, UK: Palgrave Macmillan.

Lyles, M. A. and C. R. Schwenk (1992). 'Top management, strategy and organizational knowledge structures.' *Journal of Management Studies* 29(2): 155–74.

March, J. G. (1996). 'Continuity and change in theories of organizational action.' *Administrative Science Quarterly*: 278–87.

McDougall, P. P., J. G. Covin, R. B. Robinson and L. Herron (1994). 'The effects of industry growth and strategic breadth on new venture performance and strategy context.' *Strategic Management Journal* 15: 537–54.

Miles, R. H. and C. C. Snow (1978). *Organizational Strategy, Structure and Process*. New York: McGraw Hill.

Miller, D. (1987). 'Strategy making and structure: analysis and implications for performance.' *Academy of Management Journal* 30: 7–32.

Mintzberg, H. (1994). *The Rise and Fall of Strategic Planning*. New York: Free Press.

Mintzberg, H. and J. Lampel (1999). 'Reflecting on the strategy process.' *Sloan Management Review* 40(2): 21–30.

Mintzberg, H., J. Quinn and J. Voyer (1995). *The Strategy Process*. Englewood Cliffs, NJ: Prentice Hall.

Mosalowski, E. (1993). 'A resource-based perspective on the dynamic strategy–performance relationship: an empirical examination of the focus and differentiation strategies in entrepreneurial firms.' *Journal of Management* 19(4): 819–38.

Naisbitt, J. (1994). *Global Paradox*. London: Nicholas Brealey.

Nordström, K. A. and J. Ridderstråle (1999). *Funky Business: Talent Make Capital Dance*. Falun, Sweden: BookHouse Publishing.

Normann, R. (1975). *Skapande företagsledning (Creative Corporate Management)*. Stockholm: Aldus.

Ozsomer, A., R. J. Cantalone and A. Di Benedetto. (1997). 'What makes firms more innovative? A look at organizational environmental factors.' *Journal of Business and Industrial Marketing* 12(5–6): 400–16.

Porter, M. (1980). *Competitive Strategy: Techniques for Analysing Industries and Companies*. New York: Free Press.

Porter, M. (1985). *Competitive Advantage*. New York: Free Press.

Porter, M. (1996). 'What is strategy?' *Harvard Business Review* (November–December): 61–78.

Quinn, J. B. (1995). Strategies for change. In: *The Strategy Process*. H. Mintzberg, J. B. Quinn and J. Voyer. Englewood Cliffs, NJ: Prentice-Hall.

Ruef, M. (1997). 'Assessing organizational fitness on a dynamic landscape: an empirical test of the relative inertia thesis.' *Strategic Management Journal* 18: 837–53.

Schwartz, P. (1991). *The Art of The Long View: Planning for the Future in an Uncertain World*. New York: Currency Doubleday.

Schwenk, C. R. (1995). 'Strategic decision making.' *Journal of Management* 21(3): 471–93.

Senge, P. M. (1990) *The Fifth Discipline: The Art and Practices of The Learning Organization*. New York: Currency Doubleday.

Smith, K. G., K. A. Smith, J. D. Olian, H. P. Sims Jr., D. P. O'Bannon, and J. A. Scully (1994). 'Top management team demography and process: the role of social integration and communication.' *Administrative Science Quarterly* 39: 412–38.

Teece, D. J., G. Pisano and A. Shuen (1997). 'Dynamic capabilities and strategic management.' *Strategic Management Journal* 18(7): 509–33. (Theory paper 'identifying new opportunities and organizing effectively and efficiently to embrace them are generally more fundamental to private wealth creation than strategizing'.)

Thompson, J. D. (1967). *Organizations in Action*. New York: McGraw-Hill.

Van der Heijden, K. (1996). *Scenarios: The Art of Strategic Conversation*. New York: John Wiley.

Venkatraman, N. and V. Ramanujam (1986). 'Measurement of business performance in strategy research: a comparison of approaches.' *Academy of Management Review* 11: 801–14.

Williamson, P. J. (1999). 'Strategy as options for the future.' *Sloan Management Review* (Spring 1999): 117–26.

Further Reading

Asplund, J. (1979). *Teorier om framtiden*. Stockholm: Liber.

Barker, J. (1993). *Future Edge*. William Morrow.

Coates, J. and J. Jarratt (1989). *What Futurists Believe*. Bethesda, Maryland: World Future Society.

Dewar, J. *et al.* (1993). *Assumption-Based Planning. A Planning Tool for Very Uncertain Times*. Santa Monica: RAND.

Feather, F. (1994) *The Future Consumer*. Toronto: Warwick Publishing.

Ingvar, D. and C. G. Sandberg (1985). *Det medvetna företaget. Om ledarskap och biologi*. Stockholm: Timbro.

Kelly, K. (1994) *Out of Control: The New Biology of Machines, Social Systems, and the Economic World*. New York: Addison-Wesley.

Makridakis, S. G. (1990) *Forecasting, Planning and Strategy for the Twenty-First Century*. New York: Collier Macmillan.

Morecroft, J. and J. Sterman (1994). *Modelling for Learning Organizations*. Productivity Press.

Renfro, W. L. (1993). *Issues Management in Strategic Planning*. London: Quorum.

Stewart, H. B. (1989). *Recollecting the Future: A View of Business, Technology and Innovation in the Next 30 Years*. Homewood, IL: Dow Jones-Irwin.

Index